INSTANT INTERNET ANSWERS

INSTANT INTERNET ANSWERS

Reader's Digest

CONTENTS

Introduction

The internet can make life easier, better and a lot more fun. How? In all kinds of ways. In fact, the internet is now so much part of the fabric of daily life – from doing your banking to booking a holiday – that it's becoming hard to get by without it. Things that you used to be able to do in person, by phone or post are increasingly only possible online.

And it is, after all, a fabulous invention – perhaps the greatest invention of our age – not because of the big things it can do, but because of the thousands of small ones. The internet can help you to:

- **Stay closer to friends and family.** You can send emails, catch up on Facebook and Twitter, make phone calls and video calls – all completely free.

- **Save time and money on your shopping.** You can buy pretty much anything you need online – there's no need to trawl through shops and around shopping centres. Also, many everyday things are cheaper online. What's more, you can track down rare items wherever they may be in the world.

- **Enjoy life!** So much of today's entertainment is available via the internet – music, books, TV shows and thousands of films, new and old, are just a few clicks away.

- **Find out something about absolutely anything.** The internet is an incredible resource for information – from breaking news to practical know-how. Discover how to pin down the facts, listen to the radio, learn new skills and garner tips on everything from drawing to DIY.

The best news is that the internet is simple to use. This book has been written with beginners as well as more experienced users in mind – so there's no unnecessary jargon and there are no complicated procedures to learn. Everything's explained as if you were having a conversation with a helpful, computer-savvy friend. *Instant Internet Answers* addresses the questions everyone has when they first use the internet, then goes on to cover much, much more.

Where relevant, we tell you, click by click, what to do on your computer or other device. If you need to press or select an option, we have put it in **bold text**. Here and there, you will see images like this ☰. They are intended to help you recognise the relevant icons and buttons on your screen. We've also pointed you in the direction of some of the many websites and organisations that can help you achieve what you want on the internet. And there are useful boxes with handy tips – such as how to choose between different internet providers or how to pick a strong password.

And you needn't worry about security – so long as you take the right precautions, the internet is a safe place to be. This book gives you essential safety advice whenever it crops up so that you can protect yourself. And, although there are dishonest people online – just as there are in real life – we give you tips on how to spot their scams.

All these features make *Instant Internet Answers* an essential guide for anyone who wants to make the most of all the internet has to offer. There is a virtual world of possibilities out there for you to explore and enjoy.

Note to readers

This book has been rigorously researched and written with the help of experts. Please note, however, that computers and computer programs, websites and their contents are continually being revised and updated. As a result, what you see on screen may vary from what is written here. The mention of any organisations or websites in this book does not constitute an official endorsement by Reader's Digest.

1

GETTING SET UP

Starting points

- **The internet is a marvellous means** of enriching and improving almost every aspect of your life.
- **More than a third of the world's population** are online (that is, have access to the internet). One of the highest usages is in Australia, where 83 per cent of the population uses the internet regularly.
- **There are several ways to get online,** from having a broadband connection at home to browsing on the move using your internet-connected phone ('smartphone').
- **There are simple security measures** you can use to protect your computer, and browse the internet safely.

KEY ACTIONS

- Learn how best to get connected.
- Decide between a computer, laptop, tablet or smartphone.
- Understand the difference between broadband, 3G, 4G and WiFi.
- Choose the right internet package for you.
- Find out how to set up your equipment (it's easier than you might think).
- Take the necessary steps to make your internet activity secure, at home and when you are out and about.

I hear about the internet all the time. What exactly is it, and is it the same as the web?

The terms 'internet' and 'web' are used interchangeably, but they are not exactly the same thing. The internet is a network of computers that are all linked together via cables, telephone lines and satellites – it's like a kind of giant electronic cat's cradle. The web is a vast collection of documents – consisting of words, text and video. These documents are created specifically to be viewed on a computer via a computer program called a browser. The web is accessed via the internet; you could say that it is part of the internet. But the internet comprises other elements too – such as email, for example. The internet is part of daily life for increasing numbers of people: it is used for all kinds of activities – from ordering goods and paying bills to watching videos and staying in touch with friends.

I want to use the internet, but I don't know where to start.

It is becoming easier and easier to get connected. But there's no denying that using the internet means acquiring a new set of skills – and a fair number of new words. So if you feel confused, go easy on yourself. It takes a bit of time to understand new ideas, and to find the answers to the questions that you are bound to have. Once you get connected, you will be surprised how soon it becomes an integral part of your day.

First of all, how do I get connected?

There are numerous ways to connect to the internet and various devices that you can use to do it: most obviously, a computer or laptop, a tablet or a smartphone. If you don't already have one of these, there is advice over the next few pages to help you choose. Then you will need to:

1. Find out about the different ways you can connect to the internet.

2. Choose an internet service provider (known as an ISP, for short).

3. Sign up to the right internet deal for you.

4. Receive the equipment from your ISP and set up your device (which is not difficult).

5. Install the software needed to keep your device safe (again, this is quite a straightforward process).

CHOOSING A DEVICE

I don't want to invest in a computer, but I do want to use the internet sometimes.

No problem. If accessing the internet at home is not an option for you, then there are plenty of places where you can connect, such as at your local library, which will have computers you can use. If you have some small portable internet device – such as a tablet or smartphone – then you can use it to access free internet at many cafés and other outlets.

What actually is a tablet? I am not sure.

Tablets are slim, light mini-computers that connect to the internet. They have screens that react when you tap them (touchscreens) rather than keys that you press (as on a conventional computer). The keyboard is (usually) built into the screen – and appears when needed. There are a number of button-like 'apps' on the screen and these are your starting point for whatever you want to do. There are various brands of tablet available: the Apple iPad, Samsung Galaxy Note, Google Nexus, Sony Xperia and the Amazon Kindle Fire to name some of the biggest brands.

And for that matter, what makes a phone smart?

A smartphone is like any other mobile phone in that you can make calls and send text messages. But it also connects to the internet – that's the 'smart' bit – so you can pick up emails, visit websites and the like. All the main mobile phone manufacturers now offer these devices.

What's an app? A computer application?

Yes – apps are computer programs, in many ways identical to the ones you find in the Applications folder on a desktop computer. On any smartphone or tablet you will find an internet browser app that enables you to access websites (see Chapter 2 for information on browsers). And you may also have apps that take you to a specific place on the internet: they might launch a website or open the door to a particular online store. Others do not connect to the internet, but launch a program stored on your phone or tablet, such as a game, a camera or a calendar.

Did you know?

You don't need to have a computer or tablet to use the internet. If you have a modern 'smart' TV then it has the capability to connect to the internet and allow you to visit websites, just as you would on a computer screen – you use the remote control to navigate the pages. You may also be able to watch catch-up TV episodes and play games. A less expensive option is to buy a device called a smart set-top box that you attach to a digital TV – this gives it most of the same features. Most modern games consoles also allow you to connect to the internet and visit websites using a browser (see page 45).

Which device is right for me?

Choosing between a desktop computer, laptop or tablet is the biggest decision you'll make when getting online. All modern devices are set up to receive the internet, and are pre-loaded with the software needed to use the web.

If your computer is old – in computer terms, that's five years or more – then it may not be powerful enough to run the latest versions of internet software effectively: websites will be slow to load, and some elements – such as video – may not work at all. So you may need a new machine to make the most of the internet.

Desktop computer

Advantages

A computer has a large screen, and so is good for viewing films or photos, or working on documents. A desktop is the simplest device to set up for your own comfort – you can adjust the screen to the right height for you, for example. It's much quicker to type on than a tablet – so if you are going to be writing your memoirs, say, or long emails a desktop or a laptop is the right choice. You can also store large files – the memory is much bigger than that of a tablet – and it's easier to multitask because you can have several applications open at once. Choose between a Microsoft Windows PC – which most people have – or an Apple Macintosh (a Mac), which costs more but has an aesthetically pleasing design.

Disadvantages

A computer is much bigger than a laptop or tablet, so you need space for it. It is heavy and hard to move – so will need to occupy a fixed place in your home. And it needs to be connected to a power source at all times.

Laptop or netbook

Advantages

A laptop is a portable computer, and a netbook is a smaller version of a laptop with no built-in CD/DVD drive. You can use a laptop or netbook to do a lot of typing, as with a computer, so are good options if you want to write emails, use word processing, etc. They are smaller and lighter than a computer and have a battery so you don't need to be connected to a power source all the time – you can use them in any area of the house, or take them on holiday or to work.

Disadvantages

The screen is fixed to the keyboard and can't be raised closer to eye level, which isn't good for your back if you are going to be spending long periods on it. It is heavier than a tablet, so isn't as suitable for taking out for the day – and you can't use it standing up as you can a tablet. Some people don't like using the touchpad on a laptop, but you can buy a separate mouse and connect this to the device.

Tablet

Advantages

The small design means you can just pick it up and use it wherever you are, and you can easily tuck it away in a drawer when not in use. Tablets are more limited but far simpler to use than a computer because everything is on one screen – the keyboard is cleverly designed to pop up when you need it, and you use your finger as the mouse. Tablets tend to have a longer battery life than laptops, and are good for browsing the web and for entertainment: playing games, watching films and so on. Most come with a camera so you can take snapshots or videos.

Disadvantages

The touchscreen on a tablet is delicate and if it is damaged then your whole device could stop working. A tablet is much less durable than a laptop. And you can't do as much on it as you can on a computer – for a start, typing is much slower, so it is really only suitable for short emails rather than lengthy tomes (unless you buy one with an attachable keyboard). Think of it as a device for accessing content rather than creating it.

Smartphone

Advantages

A smartphone works in the same way as a tablet – you can access the internet, receive and send emails, play games and so on, using the pop-up keyboard and your finger as a mouse. It doubles up as a camera and is the most portable option, as it is small and light and can easily be slipped into a pocket or bag. And, of course, you can make phone calls on it!

Disadvantages

The screen is very small, so you will need good eyesight to use it. Even then, it is not a good way of looking at websites or watching films for long periods.

There are so many tablets available. How do I pick between them?

The first thing to consider is the operating system (OS) that it uses. The operating system is the software that controls the device and all the applications that run on it. Apple iPads (as well as iPhones) use Apple's iOS; you can get thousands of apps from the built-in App Store if you get one of these devices. Most other tablets use Google's Android operating system; they give you access to the Google Play app store (in the case of Amazon's Kindle Fire HD, your app store is Amazon's own). A smaller number of tablets use the Windows operating system, which often come pre-loaded with similar software that you find on a PC (Word, Excel and the like). You can buy apps from the Windows Phone Store.

That's helpful. What else do I need to think about?

Memory is an important factor. You will need to consider both the storage capacity of the device, which is how many files it can hold, and also the RAM, which is the memory used to manage the applications that are open at any given time.

- Storage capacity is measured in gigabytes (GB), and can vary from 1GB to 64GB or more – 16GB is common and allows you to store approximately 20 hours of video or 9000 photos. If you think you will need more storage than that, go for a 32GB tablet at least. Some tablets have a slot for a memory card, so you can add more storage if you need it; you may also be able to plug a USB cable into the tablet, which enables you to transfer files easily to another device. And some devices offer online storage as well or instead. This saves you clogging up your device with files, but means that you have to be connected to the internet in order to access them. (See page 245 for more about online storage.)

- The RAM (short for Random Access Memory) is the temporary memory space, which is put to use when you open an app. Tablets with a large amount of RAM (say, 1GB) are able to run more apps at the same time than those with a lower RAM (512MB, or 0.5GB).

Apps and app stores

There are thousands of apps for your smartphone or tablet, and they cover almost every sphere of human interest and activity. You'll find an icon for an online app shop on your screen. You have to set up an account to use the app store – simply tap the icon and follow the instructions to do this, or go into your **Settings** menu and click **Add Account** under **Accounts**. Many apps are free but you need to put up with advertisements in order to use them; you can buy ad-free apps through your app store by entering your credit card details or using other payment options. See page 198 for more on how to download an app.

I commute, so want a tablet that will work when I am travelling.

You need one with a mobile internet connection, then. All tablets connect to the internet via WiFi (see page 31) – which means you can use them at home and in many public places. You can also download (transfer) films and books to your tablet, so you can view them when you are not connected. But if you want to browse the web or get emails when out and about, you need a tablet with a mobile internet connection. This is more expensive than a WiFi-only tablet – you pay an up-front fee or have a monthly contract.

If you want to use your device while commuting, find out how long the battery on the tablet lasts between charging. This can range from a couple of hours to more than ten – you will need a tablet with a long battery life if you are going to be using it outside your home. And here is a handy tip: the battery will last longer if you turn off the WiFi connection when you don't need it, and also close down apps that are not in use.

I am going to watch films on my tablet. Is there anything else I should look for?

The size of your tablet is a key issue. Most tablets have screens measuring 7 or 10 inches. While a smaller tablet is easier to carry around and hold, a larger screen obviously makes watching films more pleasurable. You will want a screen with a high resolution, too. Resolution is measured by the number of pixels that make up a screen – the more pixels, the sharper the image that you see. For watching films (and also for reading the type on an e-book) go for a resolution of 1280 x 800 or higher; a lower resolution is fine if you mostly want to browse the web or play simple games.

GET CONNECTED

How do I get on the internet?

There are different connection methods that provide your access to the internet – that is, different ways in which the electronic link is made between your device and all the others that make up the global network. Some of the channels involve physically plugging a computer into the long-established telephone network. Others, such as WiFi and 3G, are more like radio: you access the internet by picking up digital signals from the ether. Home broadband services – the most widespread way of accessing the internet – are a combination of the two. The signal comes down your telephone line or fibre-optic cable. It feeds into the router, which acts like a very localised radio station, broadcasting only to the various internet devices in your own home.

So, there are different ways that I can get broadband?

That's right. Broadband can come via what's called a digital subscriber line, or DSL; this is a high-speed connection that uses the same wires as your phone line. It can also come down the same line as your cable TV connection, if you have one. Or else it can be delivered via a dedicated fibre-optic cable – which is by far the fastest option, but it is not available everywhere; or broadband can be delivered via satellite, which is a good option in rural areas, where cables are scarce or uneconomical to lay. It follows that your choice of ISP may be limited by what kind of connection is available in your local area.

It sounds so complicated...

From an engineering perspective it is. But the telecoms companies that supply internet access (Internet Service Providers, or ISPs for short) are keenly interested in making it as easy as possible for customers to connect, without hiccups and without the need for technical knowledge.

What exactly is an ISP, and how do I choose one?

An ISP is a company that provides internet access in exactly the same way as your energy supplier provides gas, or your water company keeps the taps running. It is the utility that manages the digital pipeline. And as with gas and water, you can shop around. Prices and overheads vary from one company to the next, and the 'package' may not be the same from every provider. See the guide over the page for more detail on how to choose an ISP. Whichever one you choose, it'll take a few days for the broadband connection to be installed. You can pick up the necessary equipment from a retail outlet or choose to have it sent to you in the post.

What equipment do I need?

You need your own computer or other device, of course. As for the rest of the equipment, most ISPs will send everything you need by post or you can pick it up from a retail outlet. The equipment they send will probably consist of the router, which manages the internet connection inside your home; a splitter (also called a line filter) to plug into your phone line if you are getting connected that way, so that you can make calls and be online at the same time; and some cables too. There will also probably be a disk that allows you to load some necessary files onto your computer, while also giving instructions on fitting the bits together.

An ISP is a company that provides internet access in exactly the same way as your energy supplier provides gas, or your water company keeps the taps running.

Comparing ISPs

Many people get their internet service from their telephone or cable TV company. This can be a good idea since you may find a better deal if you get your phone, internet and TV services from the same company. But before you decide, think about what you actually need from an ISP. There are several things to consider.

- **The cost.** Cheapest isn't always best – there may be hidden charges, and some deals may set strict limits on the amount you can use the internet. Ask about what equipment you need to buy, any installation charges, and the monthly fee.

- **Broadband speed.** Lots of people go for the ISP that promises the fastest broadband. Be aware that the advertised speed is usually the fastest that is theoretically possible; in reality the speed is usually slower, because it depends on factors such as the number of people using the service; broadband is also often slower in the evening when more people are online. Be wary of an ISP advertising speeds significantly faster than its rivals. (See page 28 to find out how to check actual vs. advertised speeds.)

- **Limits on your usage.** Think carefully about what you want to do online. The basic package offered by your ISP may not allow you to watch much video (which requires the connection to download lots of digital information – that is, data – very quickly, and so uses up large amounts of your monthly allowance). There is no point signing up to a great deal if you end up using the internet far more than you expected, and then have to pay extra charges each month. Conversely, there's no point in paying for significantly more data allowance than you are likely to use.

- **Other terms and conditions.** Think about how long your contract is for. If you are planning to go abroad in a few months' time, or move to another part of the country, then it doesn't make sense to sign up for a two-year contract.

- **Customer service.** Consider what customer support options are offered by each ISP. Can you contact them by phone, email, messaging over the internet? What do their customers think about their service? If you already have access to the internet, type 'ISP customer service ratings' into a search engine to discover what others say about local providers – or ask someone to do this for you.

It is worth spending time comparing packages and prices offered by the various ISPs that provide internet in your area (use a friend's computer or go to a library if you are not yet online at home). There are many impartial comparison websites that enable you to weigh up the services offered by competing ISPs – type 'compare ISPs' into a search engine to find them. You just need to give details of your local area, and the site will tell you all the ISPs available to you. It may be that there aren't many ISPs covering your area, in which case your choice will be limited, but that may make your decision simpler.

Once you have used a comparison site to find out the options in your area, you can begin to investigate the providers more fully. Start by checking the reliability of the companies you are interested in. Sites such as netindex.com offer useful statistics on the quality and reliability of ISPs around the world.

Is the router set-up what is meant by 'broadband' – or is broadband something else?

'Broadband' is an umbrella term for fast internet connection via your home phone line or through a cable connection box or satellite connection – so yes. These days most people have a wireless connection – meaning that your computer does not need to be plugged into the router. The huge advantage of wireless broadband is that you can use your computer (or any internet device) anywhere in your house or in the garden: it picks up the signal from the router wherever you are so long as you are in range.

I already have broadband, but it isn't wireless. Can I change?

If you have had broadband for a while, it might be the old kind, with a cable that physically connects your computer to a modem, and then to the network (and so ties your computer to a particular spot in your home). You might want to upgrade this to a wireless system, especially if you want to buy another device such as a smartphone. You can buy the necessary router in a shop, or you can contact your ISP and ask them to provide one. They may let you have it for free if you also choose to upgrade your package with them (or threaten to leave!), so it's worth giving them a call to see what is on offer.

My phone company offers broadband. Should I go with them, or will that mean I can't make telephone calls while using broadband?

Whoever you go with, you will be able to phone and use the internet at the same time. While some broadband uses the telephone line, this does not prevent you from making and receiving telephone calls over that same phone line, as the line is split in two by the line filter supplied by your ISP. This is unlike old-fashioned dial-up internet, which monopolises the phone line when connecting to the internet, meaning you are unable to make or receive calls.

What is, or was, dial-up?

Dial-up was once the only way to use the internet. Dial-up connects to the internet using a modem, which in turn is plugged into the phone line. A modem is a device that connects you to the internet – most modern routers have a modem built in. To put it simply, dial-up is basically a phone call between two computers.

Is it a better choice than broadband?

No, there are numerous disadvantages to this now rather outmoded system. First, you are not constantly connected to the internet: you have to get your computer to make that call every time you want to go online – to collect your emails, say. Secondly, while you are online, the phone line is occupied, so you cannot make or receive telephone calls. Dial-up is also very slow compared to other more up-to-date methods: it will take you a long time to download anything such as a photo or a film clip. And, despite all its disadvantages, it is expensive, because as with any telephone call, you are paying for the time that you are connected. For all of these reasons dial-up is almost obsolete. Broadband is almost certainly your best option unless you are in a very remote area.

Dial-up is very slow compared to other more up-to-date methods

Okay, I am going to get broadband. What kind of deal do I need?

The two most important things to consider when choosing your broadband package are download quantity and speed of delivery, known in the jargon as 'bandwidth'. You remember we were saying that an ISP is like your water company? What you want your ISP to give you, metaphorically speaking, is a pipeline and a storage tank big enough for the amount of information flowing into your home (usage or quantity). And you want the flow down the pipeline to be fast enough to meet your needs second by second (speed or bandwidth).

How do I know what I will use, though?

Think about what you're going to do. Say you want to watch films over the internet. Films are extremely large computer files that need to be refreshed constantly as the film runs. For that to work on your home computer, you need a broad, fast-flowing internet-carrying 'pipe' – so you should opt for fast broadband with unlimited usage (see opposite). If you are mostly going to visit web pages and download small files, such as electronic books, to use offline (that is, when you're not connected), then anything over 500MB will be fine – this would allow you to visit 5000 web pages a month. If you want to download lots of music and videos, or listen to the radio on your device, you'll need a larger monthly download limit.

But how much is a lot?

Usage is measured in megabytes (MB) and gigabytes (GB), and a monthly allowance is often specified. Megabytes (MB) are a measure of file size equal to a million 'bytes', and a gigabyte is 1000 megabytes. There is also such a thing as a megabit (Mb). At the smallest level, a byte is equal to eight bits. It is absurd that these names, which go back to the early days of computing, are so similar and so easy to confuse – but that's just the way it is. Here is a rough guide to usage – that is, the quantity of internet you might expect to come down your pipe each month.

2GB Browsing websites and checking emails.

10GB Browsing and emailing plus listening to radio for about 80 hours or watching television for about 16 hours.

20–40GB All the above plus streaming (watching online) TV for several hours a day.

40GB+ Downloading films to watch later, or music to listen to later. One film can be 4–10GB in size, and the file sizes of music are usually stated so you can gauge your usage.

60GB+ Most of the above plus gaming or making phone calls over the internet (see page 114). Gaming can use up to 2.25GB per hour. If you make calls over the internet, then 2.4GB is used in 24 hours of call time, and if you are making video calls then the figure will be higher.

I think I can manage with a limited deal. But what happens if I use the internet more than I am allowed?

Some broadband providers offer unlimited usage as standard on all of their packages. However, if you do have a deal that caps your usage, what happens if you go over? This is normally not a big problem. Your provider should notify you (usually by email) if you are near to reaching your limit, and the charges for going over your limit are fairly reasonable. However, some providers may restrict the speed of your connection if you exceed your allowance.

It's always best to check what charges/restrictions your ISP will impose if you do exceed the limit. And if you find you are reaching your monthly limit regularly, it would be wise to discuss upgrading your package with your provider. This usually just means paying a higher monthly fee.

So that is usage. But how does speed affect my decision?

Internet speed generally starts from 1 megabit (Mb). This means that data is transferred at a rate of 1 megabit per second. (Confusingly, the 'per second' part is usually omitted, making it unclear that this is a measure of speed.) If you browse on only one computer or device at a time, then 1Mb should be fast enough. If you have numerous devices on your home network, you'll probably need 2Mb or more, because the amount of data coming down the cable will be shared between all the connected devices. If you download videos, music, play games and stream TV via the internet, you'll certainly need a fast connection as these activities jostle for space all at once. Most ISPs now offer very high speeds, such as 30Mb, 50Mb or even 100Mb through superfast fibre-optic cables.

Are those speeds guaranteed?

In reality, you may not receive such high speeds because it depends partly on what your local network is capable of – the speed is limited by the diameter and condition of the pipework between your ISP and your house, so to speak. But generally speaking, the more you pay for, the faster your experience will be.

SETTING UP

My ISP has sent the equipment. Can I set it up myself?

Most people can. It really is a pretty simple process, and it is hard to plug anything in the wrong hole, because the plugs are designed to be different from each other: if it fits, it's right; if not, it's wrong. Once you've connected everything, it's a good idea to take a photo (or draw a picture) of the leads that go into your router and your computer, so if you ever have to unplug them you know how to connect them back up again quickly.

Is there anything else I'll need to do?

Once you have set up the equipment, you will have to configure your computer or other device to connect to the internet. Your ISP should give you all the information that you need to do this – if you are using a computer or laptop and have received a CD, then put the CD in and follow the on-screen instructions to complete the broadband installation.

There is no CD. What should I do?

Often a CD is not needed. Your computer, tablet or smartphone will automatically search for a connection and find it. All you then need to do is to select the right connection by looking for your home router's name, or SSID (short for Service Set Identity). This will be listed on your router and/or in your paperwork from your ISP. Then type in your password (which you'll find on your router and/or in the paperwork from your ISP). Click OK and away you go.

My computer doesn't seem to be searching for a connection?

In this case, you can manually connect to your network. In Windows, go to **Control Panel**, then **Network and Internet** and select **Connect** to a network. On a Mac, click on the Apple icon, then **System Preferences** (under **Internet and Wireless**), then **Network**. From here you can select your network name, enter the password and connect.

It all sounds too complicated. Can I get someone to set up my internet?

Yes, of course. Lots of people call on a tech-savvy friend or relative to do this for them. And some ISPs offer a service where an engineer can come to your house to set everything up for you. You will have to pay an additional fee for this, though.

My connection was fine when I set it up but now the internet isn't working. What do I do?

First, check the power is switched on to your router and all the cables are plugged in – to your phone line or cable box and to the router. Next, turn your router off then on again, then restart your computer and see if this clears the problem.

Slow broadband? Speed it up

The internet delivers information in an instant… theoretically. But you may find that your internet is very slow. If things aren't working as they should, there are various ways of improving them.

First, check what speed you signed up to. This is the speed of internet that you ought to be getting – so long as the network in your local area can handle it. If the cabling where you live can't manage the internet speed you subscribed to, then your internet connection won't be as fast as your ISP promises – at least not until the cables in your area are upgraded. Next, check the speed of your broadband, to find out if it is as slow as you think – there are several websites, such as speedtest.net, where you can measure the speed of your broadband by following some simple instructions.

If your broadband speed is much slower than advertised, talk to the customer services department of your ISP. It may be that there is a technical problem with your router; if so, they may send a technician to fix it. Or, if you've been on a slow internet speed package for a long time, they may offer you an upgrade for little or no extra cost.

There are several other reasons why your internet speed could be running slower than expected. It might be your computer, not the broadband, that is slow. Check that your antivirus software is up to date and functioning: viruses can clog your machine and make it sluggish (see page 36). Check that your router and your browser are also up to date (you can download the latest versions of most of the widely used browser programs for free).

Turn off any applications that you are not using. If you are on a PC, go to the **Task Manager** (press **Ctrl+Alt+Delete**) and check that none of the listed programs is using up a large part of your bandwidth. Some of them may be unnecessary, or not in use by you. If in doubt, ask an expert. Don't allow applications such as live TV streaming to go on in the background when you are not watching, because they will slow your connection and use up your monthly allowance. If you go over your monthly allowance, your ISP can restrict the speed of internet usage in order to penalise you: check that this is not the case.

It is possible that your WiFi is causing the problem. Connect your computer or laptop with a cable to the router to see if you get faster speeds. If you do, then the wireless connection is the issue. If so, then try these measures:

- **Buy an antenna booster or** a wireless repeater. Either of these will boost the signal or range of the WiFi within your home.

- **Protect your WiFi with a strong password** (see page 38), so that you are not sharing your connection with your neighbours or anyone passing by. You should do this for security reasons, of course, but you will also get better speeds if no one is piggybacking on your WiFi.

- **If you use DSL (telephone) broadband,** make sure that the router is plugged into the master telephone socket. Avoid using extension leads to connect from your phone socket to the router as these will slow down the connection. If you must use one, make it as short as possible. Do check your phone lines since damaged or old wiring can be the cause of a slow connection. And make sure that you have a splitter/line filter plugged into every phone socket in the house. If not, this, too, could be the cause of slow speed and disconnections.

My connection is still not working.

The next step is to check your network connection. In Windows, from the **Start** menu, open the **Control Panel** and click on **Network** and **Internet** or **Network Options**. Depending on your version of Windows, all of the possible network connections (that is, WiFi and other networks) will be listed here, or you will need to make one more click on **View Network Status** and **Tasks** to get there. You will see the name of your router listed – click on that. Once you have opened this connection, try clicking on **Disable** to disconnect, then on **Enable** to reconnect. This sometimes fixes a connection problem.

If you have a Mac, go to **System Preferences** (on the **Apple** menu), **Network**, then click **Assist Me** then **Diagnostics**. A pop-up window will appear with instructions on how to investigate and fix the problem.

If after doing all these checks your internet is still not working, you should ring your ISP and report the problem. It may be that there is an issue with the internet service to your area, or they may be able to help you diagnose and fix the problem.

The connection keeps failing. What is going on?

This shouldn't be happening. If you've done all of the above checks and you are still having problems, then there is a wider issue. This could be with your equipment (such as your router or cables) or with the local network. Either way, ring your ISP and explain the problem and what you have done to investigate it.

What will the ISP do?

They may send out an engineer to check your equipment or check your local network and fix it. Sometimes, if you have an old router or separate modem and router, the equipment may not be able to cope with the faster speeds now available or with the number of devices trying to connect in your household. Your ISP may supply a new combined router/ modem that will give you better service.

ALL ABOUT WIFI, 3G AND 4G

What exactly is WiFi – is it something that comes with broadband?

WiFi is something that tends to come with broadband – but it is more than that. WiFi (it stands for 'wireless fidelity' and is a lame pun on 'hifi') is the term for a small wireless network – like the one that you have in your home once you install wireless broadband. The same networks exist in all kinds of public places – cafés, yes, but also libraries, airports, railway stations, hotels, sports centres, pubs... When you are in these places you can log into their wireless network (usually for free, though you may have to register in some way), and gain access to the internet that way.

The WiFi symbol looks like a kind of fan which is black when the connection is working, or else like a bar graph. It will appear at the top right of your screen if you are on a Mac; at the bottom right if you are on a PC. If some of the bars are grey, that means the signal is not as strong as it could be (which might mean your connection is slow). If all the bars are grey, that means the device knows you have WiFi, but the connection has been lost temporarily.

Can all mobile phones connect to the internet?

All modern smartphones can. To check whether your smartphone or tablet is connected, tap the **Settings** icon – the name of your network should appear next to the option that says **WiFi**, or it will say 'No connection'. Tap here, and you should get a list of active WiFi connections in the vicinity. If yours is there, tap it to get connected. If not, then your connection has failed, and you will need to restart the router (see page 27).

What if I'm using my smartphone or tablet on the street – how do I access the internet there?

There are many places where you can get free internet access when you are out – these WiFi hot spots, as they are known, include cafés, libraries and some public transport. If there is no available WiFi network, a smartphone or tablet can still access the internet through a different system called 3G or (the newer version) 4G, which is part of the mobile phone network (you generally pay for this through a monthly contract).

You may have heard scary stories about people who have run up a huge monthly bill when their phones have accessed the internet while abroad. This is possible, but it happens only when 'Data Roaming' is turned on. Go into your **Settings** menu, and look for **Mobile** or **Mobile Networks** to turn it off before you go. You can still use the internet by connecting to a free WiFi network. And while connected to WiFi you can make free phone calls home using apps such as Skype (see page 114) and Viber (see page 117).

Can I use 3G and 4G with a laptop, or is it just for smartphones and tablets?

Yes you can. You can obtain an internet signal from the mobile-phone network, rather than the WiFi network, by using a dongle. This is a small device about the size of a key ring, which plugs into your laptop. It acts as a kind of aerial that allows you to connect to the internet by picking up the signal from the mobile telephone network. However, this is generally a more expensive way to connect to the internet than through home WiFi, and so is designed for those who need to use the internet a lot when out, such as business users. If you don't use the internet much when away from home, stick with just your home WiFi and WiFi signals from cafés and the like.

To get an internet signal from the mobile-phone network on a laptop, you need to plug in a dongle.

Can I use 3G and 4G at home instead of getting WiFi?

This is possible but may work out more expensive and perform less well than a broadband internet (WiFi) connection, depending on the availability of broadband in your area. Another option is mobile broadband. This could be comparable or even cheaper in price, but again the bandwidth is unlikely to be as good.

Mobile broadband, or MiFi, makes use of a mobile wireless router that transmits 3G and 4G signals from the cellular (mobile-phone) network rather than a WiFi broadband connection from your phone or cable line. MiFi routers are usually a lot smaller than a WiFi router and are portable – so they can be taken out of the home very easily, meaning your network can travel with you. This can mean you use up more bandwidth and so require a more expensive monthly usage limit than with home broadband/WiFi. One downside to MiFi is that it usually has slower maximum speeds than home broadband with WiFi, but that may well improve in the future.

ALL ABOUT SECURITY

I am worried about being online – how do I stay secure?

Lots of people worry about their online security, and with good reason. It's true that the internet can be a source of many scams – and there are always scare stories in the newspapers about viruses infecting machines and hackers accessing people's personal information online. So it would be easy to think that browsing the net is a dangerous activity. But staying safe online is the same as staying safe anywhere – take the right precautions from the start, use your common sense, and you can protect yourself from problems. In the same way that you lock up your home and shut the windows when you go out, your computer needs some basic security to guard against intruders.

As soon as you get connected, you need to put in place some security systems. But don't think that you are on your own in trying to protect your internet device – your ISP, the computer manufacturers and software engineers are continually striving to improve security, and automatically build in protection to help you.

What do I need?

Your computer has three lines of defence (or should have). Each of them helps keep your computer safe from attack. The three systems are the firewall, antivirus software and an up-to-date operating system.

First, what's a firewall?

If you are connected to the internet via a home broadband router, it will almost certainly have some protective software called a firewall built in. When you are online, you connect to other computers to access their services. Conversely, other computers on the internet can access services presented by your computer. The firewall acts as a digital barrier, blocking access to your computer unless you allow it. It is a bit like a nightclub bouncer, standing between the computers in your home and the troublemakers of the net.

How does it work?

It monitors all communication coming from the internet, allowing outsiders to access only the services you tell it are okay. This generally means that they are blocked from accessing your computer unless they are responding to a request from it. Modern desktop and laptop computers generally have a firewall built in, too. This allows you to protect yourself even if you are using a public WiFi network – for example, if you are using WiFi in a hotel or an airport departure lounge.

Firewalls also help thwart attacks by 'worms', a kind of malicious software that is spread from one device to another across a network. So it's a good idea to ensure that your computer's internal firewall is switched on (enabled), to reduce the chance of a worm spreading to all the devices that use your home broadband connection.

How do I check my firewall's turned on?

You will find your firewall settings in the **Control Panel** (Windows) or **System Preferences** (Mac) in the **Apple** menu, under **Security**. Make sure the firewall is **On**.

As alternatives to the built-in firewall, there are a number of free and paid-for firewalls that you can download from websites – ZoneAlarm (zonealarm.com) and Comodo (comodo.com) are two internet-security companies that offer these. These firewalls offer slightly better security than your built-in firewall but they are necessary only if you think your computer is at significant risk of attack. If you do install a different firewall, make sure that you have only one enabled on your computer; otherwise the firewalls will clash and not work effectively.

Does a firewall protect my computer against everything?

No, firewalls do a lot but they do not protect against a lot of malware – malicious software – including viruses and spyware (see below). That is why you also need to install antivirus software.

What does antivirus software do?

Good antivirus software helps to protect against viruses, Trojans and spyware as well as worms.

- **A virus** is a software program that can spread from computer to computer like a disease. It infects your computer and can cause harm and destroy your files. Viruses are spread by opening infected files that you download from a website or receive via email.

- **A Trojan** is a particular kind of virus that is designed to steal your personal information.

- **Spyware** enters your computer and 'spies' on what you're doing. It does this by, for example, logging the keys you type and thereby stealing your passwords and other personal information.

Before choosing any antivirus software, check that it is effective against viruses, Trojans, worms and spyware.

How do I get this software?

Antivirus software is produced by many companies. As well as blocking malware, it will scan your computer for existing viruses and remove them. There are many different antivirus software brands available to download free from the internet, including avast! Free Antivirus, AVG Antivirus Free and Panda Cloud Antivirus Free. Make sure you download these from the official website, such as avast.com, avg.com and pandasecurity.com. If you prefer, you can buy antivirus software from a computer shop. Since new viruses are being created all the time, it is important to keep your antivirus protection updated. Most antivirus software updates automatically, so you shouldn't need to worry about remembering to do this.

My friend says I don't need antivirus software if I have a Mac. Is that true?

Macs are traditionally less vulnerable to attack. This is partly because fewer people have them – it makes sense for criminals to go after Windows computers because there are so many more of them that a virus could reach. But that's not to say that Macs aren't at risk. It's still a good idea to get antivirus software, and Mac users, like everyone else, should be sure to download software only from known sources to help keep their computers safe.

What's an operating system, and why do I need it to be up to date?

The manufacturers are constantly striving to make their software as secure as possible – they pinpoint any weak points, and create updates to fix them. This means that the latest version of an operating system – the program that makes your computer run – is likely to be more secure than an older one. So make sure that you install any updates to your operating system when they become available.

How do I do that?

On a Mac or a PC, you'll get pop-up messages on screen telling you that software updates are available, and you then just click OK to download them. To check whether updates are available in Windows, go to the **Control Panel** and find the **Security** section then click on **Windows Updates** to find the **Check for Updates** option. On a Mac, from the **Apple** menu select **Software Update** to check for updates.

What more can I do to make my home broadband secure?

It is vital to protect your broadband connection with a strong password. This should be done for you by the ISP: routers always come with a preset password, and it's usually a strong password (that is, a random mixture of upper- and lower-case letters and numbers or other characters). If it is not, then change it (use the safe password guidelines on page 76).

You have probably noticed a whole host of other WiFi networks come up on the list of WiFi connections available to your home computer. This is a list of your neighbours' networks, and they can probably see yours, too. If the network is accessed by a password, it will have a little padlock symbol next to it – and only people who know the password will be able to access it. So long as you password-protect it, your WiFi is relatively safe from hackers (people who use weaknesses in a computer system to gain access to its data) – and from opportunist neighbours who piggyback on your network and so use up your monthly data download allowance.

I have a strong password. Is there anything else?

Make sure your computer is not set up to connect automatically to any available WiFi network. If it is, it could connect to networks other than your own – networks that you know nothing about, and that might be unsecure. Not all computer systems allow automatic connection, but it's worth checking that this option is disabled on your system.

In Windows, go to **Network Connections** from the **Start** menu and then **Control Panel**. Right-click on the **Wireless Network Connection** icon and click on **Properties**. Select the name of your router and then click on **Advanced**. Choose the **Access point (infrastructure) networks only** tab and make sure the box that says **Automatically connect to non-preferred networks** is not ticked.

On a Mac, from the **Apple** menu go to **System Preferences** and select **Network**. Make sure that the **Network Name** lists your router, and that **Ask to join new networks** is ticked.

I am using a tablet. Are there any security steps I should take?

Tablets and smartphones don't usually have a firewall or antivirus software but have other precautions already in place – for example, iPhones don't allow any software to be downloaded unless it is from the official App Store. Whatever phone or tablet you have, it is wise to download only from the trusted marketplaces (see page 16). It is also a good idea to download a specially designed security app for your phone – such as Avast! Free Mobile Security – available from your app store.

I use the computer at the library. Is that safe?

Don't use a public computer for financial transactions, or to send emails with your bank details in them. You cannot know whether a hacker has accessed the machine and installed software that tracks your keystrokes. Someone could do this, and gain access to all your passwords and usernames. It's best to stick to general browsing only when you are on a computer that is publicly accessed. Always log out at the end of the session.

What about WiFi? Is it safe to use free WiFi when I am out and about?

That's a good question. It's certainly convenient to use WiFi but it is difficult to know whether a public WiFi connection is secure, so it is wise to take some precautions before you do so. And as with a public computer, it is best not to carry out financial transactions on a public WiFi network – save them until you are on your secured home connection. If you do have to type in your credit card number, then check that you are using a secure website: check that the web address begins with https rather than the usual http (the 's' stands for 'secure'). (See page 54 for more about secure websites.)

What do I need to do to use WiFi safely?

Here are some basic security steps to take before using WiFi:

- First, go into the **Settings** menu and look at the WiFi settings to make sure your smartphone or tablet isn't set up to connect automatically to free WiFi whenever it is available – look for an option to **disable auto-connecting** and turn it off. If you can't see this option then it doesn't exist and you're safe. Otherwise you could be using free WiFi without even realising it, and without knowing the source of that free WiFi.

- In a café or other reputable place, check the exact name of the WiFi network with staff. That way you know you are definitely connecting to the right one, and not a look-alike network set up by hackers to access your personal information (this is quite easily done). Even then, there is always a slim chance that a member of staff could also be a hacker – so you should still limit what you do in public.

- If you are using a laptop, make sure your firewall is turned on when you're using a public network as it will filter what is allowed to pass through the 'wall' from the internet to your device. Make sure that your antivirus software and your operating system are up to date.

- Remember to use 'strong' passwords – ideally, a mixture of letters, numbers and characters – for any websites you use. Don't use the same password for different sites – if one gets discovered, your other sites are vulnerable. (See page 76 for advice on creating strong passwords.)

- Disconnect from the WiFi if you don't need to be online.

That's all useful. Is there anything else I can do to protect myself?

One important thing. If you have several devices you probably allow sharing of music, printers and other files between your devices when you are on your home network. When using a public WiFi connection, you should disable these sharing settings. To do this, go to the **Control Panel** (Windows) or **System Preferences** (Mac) and untick all the sharing options.

2

BROWSING THE INTERNET

Starting points

- **The world wide web** consists of more than a billion websites created by individuals and organisations all over the world.
- **A web page may have** text, graphics, pictures, video, sound, and links to other web pages. A website is a collection of closely related pages.
- **You access the web using a browser.** This is software that enables you to find and use websites.
- **Every web page has a unique address** called a uniform resource locator (URL). This is how a browser finds it.
- **You can search through** millions of pages on the web in just a few seconds using websites known as search engines.

KEY ACTIONS

- Get the most out of your browser.
- Find the information you want – fast.
- Set your home page.
- Browse safely and protect your privacy.
- Speed up a slow browser.

BROWSING BASICS

How do I get onto the web?

You use a browser. This is a computer program that can seek out any one of the millions of web pages out there, and then display them on your computer screen. It is your window on the web. To put it another way, if you think of the web as a kind of vast library (as the term 'web page' implies) then a browser is like a kind of all-knowing librarian who can instantly direct you to the book you want – indeed the very chapter or paragraph or sentence within the book.

Words and pictures were once just about all that the web could manage – but it has developed rapidly to the point where it is capable of far more than that. You can view films and TV shows, listen to digital radio and download music, communicate with individuals or large groups of people, buy almost anything you can think of. So in fact the web is no longer merely a hushed library – albeit an almost limitless one. It is now more like a digital city containing crowd-filled squares, bustling shops and market places, endless cinemas and concert halls. The browser on your computer gives you access to all of this and more.

How do I get a browser?

You almost certainly already have browser software installed on your machine. It has been a standard program on all new computers for some years now. If your computer is more than, say, five years old, then you may find that your browser is very slow. Most likely, however, your computer is relatively new and ready to start. For a PC running Microsoft Windows, the default browser (the one that comes pre-installed) is Internet Explorer, while Apple computers come with Safari. All smartphones, netbooks and tablets are equipped with a browser.

A browser is like a kind of all-knowing librarian who can instantly direct you to the book you want.

So I just use the browser that comes with my computer?

Not necessarily. It is easy to install another browser on your machine – there are several free browsers available online, including Firefox and Google Chrome. See Which browser? on page 53 for details on where you can find these browsers, how to get them onto your computer and why you might want to use them.

How do I use it?

Your computer needs to be connected to the internet for your browser to work. You launch your browser in the same way that do any other application on your computer.

- On a Windows PC: if there is an Internet Explorer icon on your screen, click on that to open it. If not, click **Start** at the bottom left of your screen. Click on the **Internet Explorer** icon. The program will load, opening a window on your screen.

- On a Mac: click on the browser icon on your desktop (it should be in the dock, which is a column at the left or bottom of your screen). If it is not there, then go to your Applications folder, find your browser in the list, and double-click on it.

- On a tablet or smartphone: tap the browser icon once.

Is the browser on my tablet the same as the one on my computer?

Smartphone and tablets all come with a browser – Google Chrome for Android phones, Internet Explorer for Windows phones, Safari for Apple devices and Kindle Silk for the Kindle Fire, to name some of the most popular ones. The screen is obviously much smaller on a tablet or phone, and to suit this the browser is a streamlined version of what you see on a computer. But whichever browser you are using on your tablet or phone, it will have a combined address and search bar, a stop/refresh button, and back and forward buttons. As on a computer browser, there will also be other useful features, including a facility to open several pages at once so that you can multitask.

Know your browser

When you open your browser, you see a web page, with icons and menus at the top. You don't need to know what they all do in order to start browsing – but they can all help you make the most of using the web. They look different depending on the browser you are using, but they all perform the same basic functions. These are the ones that you will need straight away.

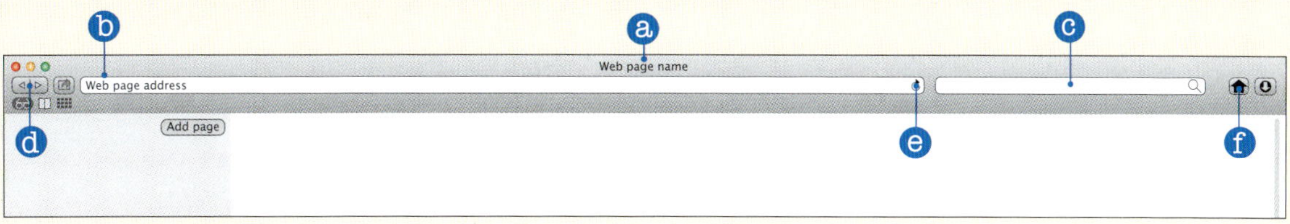

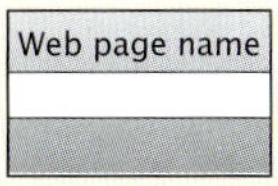

a Title bar At the very top of the screen, you will see the name of the web page you are viewing, possibly with a little logo image next to the name.

b Address bar The long box at the top of your screen shows you the address of the web page you are on. This is where you type in a web address of a page you want to visit, usually starting with http://.

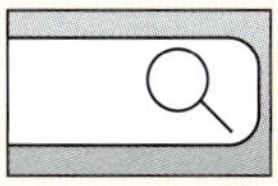

c Search bar When you don't know the web address you want, you type keywords into the search bar. On some browsers, the search bar is the same as the address bar; on others, it is next to it.

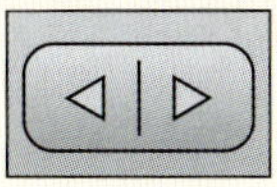

d Back/forward arrows These let you switch back and forth to websites you have been using, in the order you visited them.

e Stop/refresh buttons Use the stop button (usually an X) at the far right of the address bar if a website takes a long time to load or you change your mind about visiting it. If a page is slow to load, press the refresh button (an arrow or arrows forming a circle that appears in place of the X) and it may swiftly appear.

f Home page If you have browsed to other pages and want to return to your home page, you can do so by clicking on this house-shaped button.

I've started my browser and it has taken me to a website that I'm not interested in. Why has that happened?

When you launch your browser, you are always taken to the same page – your home page. This is set up automatically by the browser's manufacturer, and is often their own page – Internet Explorer starts with a Microsoft page, for example. It is easy to change your home page if you want to – you might want it to take you to, say, a current affairs site if the first thing you do each day is catch up on the news. There's information about how to do this on page 62.

How do I get to a website I do want to visit then?

If you know its web address, you can type it into the address bar – this is the long white box at the top of the screen – and then press **Enter/Return** on your keyboard to load the page (or tap **Go** if you are on a phone or tablet). On some browsers, when a page is loading the address bar will turn blue from left to right. This should happen within a second or so, but may take longer depending on the complexity of the page you are loading and the speed of your connection.

It's a really long web address. Do I have to type in the whole thing?

You can forget the http:// for a start – just type in the name from www. If you are visiting the website of a major company, then you don't have to bother with the www bit either. Say, for example, that you want to visit www.amazon.com. Just type 'amazon' and the correct website address should pop up. Press **Enter/Return** to go there and the browser will either load the page directly or take you to a search results page from where you can click through to the right site.

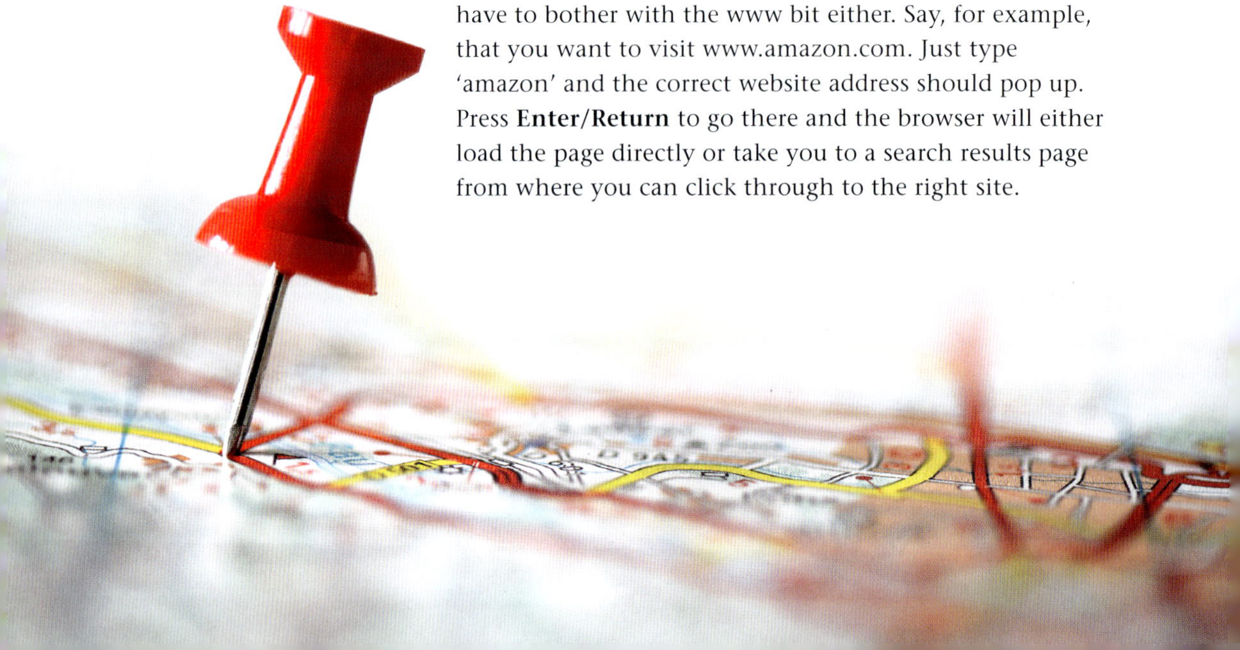

That's great. Any other tips?

Your browser is primed for speed, and it tries to anticipate the website you want based on the websites you have visited previously. When you start typing, it provides a list of suggested websites – which is updated with each character that you type. So, for example, you may only need to type the characters 'rea' for www.readersdigest.com to pop up in a list below the address bar or in the address bar itself, depending on what browser you are using. Click on the right address, or press **Enter/Return** if it is in the address bar.

Another handy feature of your browser is that it allows you to remember sites that you visit often by setting them as **Favorites** (called **Bookmarks** on some browsers). This turns the web address into a button on your toolbar – a menu at the top of the browser – that you just click once to go straight there. See page 70 for more information on how to do this. Also, as you browse around a website, you will often find a hyperlink – click on this and a new web page will swiftly load.

What's a hyperlink?

Web pages are usually connected to many others via 'hyperlinks' ('links' for short) – this is one of the things that makes navigating the web a quick and easy process. A website – which is a collection of closely related web pages – will have links to its other pages, and often to other websites as well. When you click on a hyperlink, you are automatically taken to the related web page.

Why are web addresses so complicated?

Each web page has a unique address. This is called its URL (short for 'uniform resource locator'). The URL may look long and complex but it is not as confusing as it may seem at first – the convention for naming websites is actually quite straightforward. And it is just a way to help the computer find and retrieve the web page you want.

Here is a breakdown of a typical website address:

- **A web page URL starts with the characters http://** This is its 'protocol', a reference to the set of rules that allows computers to speak to each other. If you enter a URL and omit the http:// prefix, the browser will still assume you are looking for a web page.

- **The address normally continues with www.** This stands for 'world wide web', the part of the internet that contains websites (see page 11 for an explanation of the difference between the internet and the web).

- **Then you have the name of the organisation** that owns the site, or a name that indicates what the site is about. This is called the domain name. If the website is a company or an organisation, then this part of the address will be the company's or organisation's name, or a version of it. The name could also just be an indication of the subject of the site. So, for example, the simply named www.davidbowie.com is the singer's own site; www.bowiewonderworld.com is a fan site dedicated to him. The obvious and simple domain name is more likely to be 'official', since organisations (and celebrities) want people to find their site easily or to be able to guess its address.

- **Finally, there is a suffix** that indicates what type of organisation owns the site, and perhaps where it is in the world. You may also see more words or numbers after the suffix – this is the unmemorable gobbledegook that defines a page within a site.

Here are the most common suffixes you get at the end of a web address:

.com can be used by anyone in the world, originally intended for companies
.gov US government, or followed by a country code for other countries
.edu US educational establishment, or followed by a country code for other countries
.net can be used by anyone in the world, originally intended for networks within organisations and companies
.org can be used by anyone in the world, originally intended for organisations such as charities or special-interest groups

There may also be a two-letter country code after the suffix. For example:

.au stands for Australia
.cn for China
.in for India
.nz for New Zealand
.uk for the United Kingdom

Go to www.iana.org and follow the links to what is called the root zone database to see a full list of country codes. Be aware though that a country suffix doesn't automatically mean that the website originates in that country; it simply means that somebody has chosen it for their website.

As the web grows ever larger, more suffixes will have to be coined. In the near future you can expect to start seeing regional suffixes – in 2014, London, UK, became the first city to get its own suffix (.london) – and there are also subject suffices, such as .music (.tv is already taken, for the country Tuvalu).

How do I know a link when I see one?

They are usually quite obvious. A link may be:

- text that is underlined
- text that is a different colour
- an image
- an icon
- a button.

If you want to see if something is a link, let your cursor hover over it. If it is a link, the mouse arrow usually turns into a hand with a pointing finger. Click now, and another page loads in an instant. Sometimes a link takes you to a different point on the same web page rather than to a new web page.

Is it safe to click on a link?

Most links you come across are fine, and they are one of the main ways to navigate the internet, so you can't avoid them. But they are also used by fraudsters. If a link seems odd to you in any way, then don't click it. Here are a few types of links you should definitely avoid.

- **Ads that promise the impossible** such as a get-rich-quick scheme, instant ways to look ten years younger or a notification that you have just won a prize (often for being the zillionth visitor to a website). These are almost certainly fake.

- **A suggestion that you download a new piece of software** – unless you know that is what you want to do, and you are using a trusted site.

- **Warning messages** telling you your computer is at risk unless you click: they are likely to take you to a site where your computer *will* be at risk.

- **A link in an email that appears to be from a bank** and asks you to enter your bank or security details. Your bank will never ask for these details in this way.

- **A link in an email from a stranger** or from someone you know but with a message that isn't in his or her usual style (a hacker could have accessed your email account). See page 110 for more on links in emails.

Which browser?

There are some good arguments for changing your browser or using more than one, because their features vary, and some are easier to use than others.

The best way to decide on the browser that suits your needs is to download a couple and try them out – the ones listed here are all free. The icons and layout may not look quite the same as those in your built-in browser, and may take a little getting used to. But all browsers function on the same principles, have the same basic features and can take you wherever you want to go on the web. These are the four most popular browsers:

Chrome Google's browser has a smooth, minimal look that is designed to waste as little of your screen space on its controls as possible. There are lots of extras that you can add to the basic browser if you want them. Chrome can be downloaded for Macs and Windows PCs from google.com/chrome.

Firefox This browser comes from Mozilla, an organisation that provides free software. It has a clean, uncluttered design, with good security features. It runs on Macs as well as Windows PCs, and is available from mozilla.org.

Internet Explorer This is Microsoft's browser, and is built into Windows. It has a streamlined design and is simple to use. To get Internet Explorer or to update to the latest version, go to microsoft.com/ie. It is not available for Macs.

Safari The default browser on Macs, as well as on other Apple devices such as iPhones and iPads. Lots of people like Safari because it has built-in features such as Reader (see page 56) to make browsing easier. If you use a Windows PC but like the look of Safari, you can download it: go to support.apple.com and follow the links for downloads and then Safari.

Always go to the manufacturer's official website to download software, and follow the instructions. When you open a new browser for the first time, you will be asked if you want to import your settings from your previous browser. It will save you time if you say yes. Browsers are constantly being updated, so be sure to get the latest version and any updates as soon as they become available.

How can I check whether a link is safe?

If you are unsure about a link then first check the address by hovering over the link: the address will come up at the bottom left of your browser. Check that it's what you would expect it to be; if it is different from the link (or slightly odd – amzon rather than amazon, for example), then you should be wary. Once you are on the website, check the address bar, which displays the web address – is it the right one?

Don't worry too much if you have clicked onto a fake website by accident – so long as you have a good antivirus software running (see page 36) then clicking on bogus links shouldn't cause you a problem.

WHEN IS A SITE SECURE?

Never type in personal or financial information unless you are sure you are on a secure website. It is easy to tell: a secure site may have a small padlock in the address bar and the address always starts https rather than http. The 's' indicates that information from the website is encrypted (scrambled), and so can't be intercepted by a third party as it travels over the internet.

Improving readability

The web page takes up more space than I can see on my screen. How can I look at the rest of it?

A web page often has more information than you can see on one screen. The page is anchored to the top left of your screen, so to see more you need to scroll downwards, and sometimes to the right as well.

You do this in the same way that you move around, say, a Word document. There is a scroll bar to the right and sometimes at the base of the web page. Place your cursor on the scroll bar, then click and drag to move the screen in the right direction. Press the arrow keys on your keyboard to move up and down the web page; these will also allow you to move right and left.

The text on websites is much too small for me to read.

It's simple to change the size and appearance of the text that appears on websites, and this will make it a lot easier to read. On most browsers, this is just a case of zooming in and out: hold down the **Ctrl** or **Cmd** key at the same time as pressing the + or – buttons. On tablets and smartphones, you place your finger and thumb on the screen and move them in and out of a 'pinch' position. And if you want to set just the text to the size you need, you can do that too:

- If you are using Internet Explorer, select an appropriate text size directly from the **View** option on the menu bar.
- For Chrome, click on the three-lines icon ☰ next to the web address bar and select **Settings**, then **Advanced settings** and select a larger font size under **Web Content**.
- In the Firefox **Tools** menu bar, go to **Options**, then **Preferences**, then **Fonts and colours** where you can specify the desired font size.
- Mac users browsing with **Safari** can find similar controls in the menu bar at Safari: click on **Preferences** and then select **Appearance**.

I still find most websites too busy. I'm really just interested in the words.

Safari has a handy little feature called Reader – you will find it at the right-hand end of the address bar. Click on this and all the ads and other paraphernalia are stripped away – leaving you with a much cleaner, more readable page. Other browsers don't include this facility as standard, but in most cases you can download a similar 'add-on' – an extra feature, which is sometimes called an extension or a plug-in – called Readability, which you can use in the same way.

That sounds really useful. How do I get Readability?

Go to the website readability.com and follow the instructions to download it to your browser. The site recognises which browser you are on, and automatically directs you to a compatible version of the software. You will also find it – and many others add-ons – at your browser's online store (see page 72 for more about downloading add-ons).

I am looking at a website on my phone, but it doesn't fit in the screen.

These days most websites are set up so that they can easily be read on a smartphone or tablet as well as a computer – the web page adjusts to the size of your screen automatically. If you are finding the website impossible to view, then you are probably on the desktop site – that is, a page designed to be viewed on the wide screen of a computer rather than the narrow, upright rectangle of the phone. There should be an option to switch to the specially configured mobile site somewhere on the page. Many popular websites – Facebook, for example – offer a free app that you can download to your phone or tablet to make it easier to use the site. This is worth doing if it is one that you visit often from a mobile device – go into the app store on your mobile device to find it.

Using a search engine

I am not sure what website I want. I just need information.

The great thing about the internet is that you can find out almost anything – provided you know where to look. And a search engine – a vast electronic index of web pages – is designed to help you do that. You simply type significant words (keywords) into the search box, and the search engine loads a list of sites that may have the information you are searching for. It ranks them for you, too – with the most likely contenders first. Search engines are continuously updated, to ensure that their listings are current.

Most search engines are global companies but because you are most likely to be interested in information from your own region, they offer country-specific search engines – such as google.co.in for India and google.com.au for Australia.

Choose your search engine

Search engines are a basic tool for any web user. Here is a brief guide to five of the best-known and most useful.

Google This is by far the most popular search engine – so much so that 'to google' has become a common verb. Google offers many types of search: you can choose to search just images, or only shops. It has a predictive text function, meaning that it tries to guess what you are looking for as you type.

Yahoo! This is good for searching videos online and, like Google, has an image search and other facilities. It also has a tool that allows you to search for businesses in your area. You can customise Yahoo! to show the kinds of news stories that you are likely to be interested in.

Ask.com This site has a smaller database than other search engines, but offers a different way of searching – once you have typed in your keywords, it suggests popular questions and answers related to your search.

Bing Microsoft's search engine. It features a picture of the day (making it a fun choice for your home page). As with Google, you can search for images and you can preview pages by hovering over the results with your mouse.

DuckDuckGo This search engine is growing in popularity because it is one of the few that does not keep track of data entered by its users. You can choose to view results with Web of Trust ratings activated – this means that results will be colour coded to suggest whether users have rated them as safe to click on or not.

What are keywords?

They are significant words or phrases that are likely to appear in any article or website containing the information that you want. Say you want to find information on why your heel hurts when you walk – your keywords could be 'heel pain walking'.

Where do I type the keywords?

There are two ways of entering keywords into a search engine:

- Depending on your browser, you type the keywords or question into the address bar or a separate search bar to the right of it, and press **Enter**.
- Alternatively, go to the search engine's own website, where you will find some useful ways of narrowing or broadening your search.

Once you start typing, some search engines try to anticipate what you are looking for: a list of popular searches will appear below the search box as you start to type. If one of these matches your search, you can click on it rather than continue to type.

What about local information? Say I want to find a garden centre near me?

No problem. The web works like a constantly updated directory of local services: you can track down a garden centre, pet shop, carpenter, builder or any other company in an instant. Most businesses now have a website giving details of their services and contact information. To find the one you want, simply type in the type of company or service – 'garden centre' or 'plumbing' plus the name of your town or area. A list of local suppliers will appear in the results and, depending on the search engine you use, there may also be a map with pointers showing where they are.

Can I trust the information I find on the web?

Anyone can produce a website and so the information on any given website is no more or less reliable or rigorous than the person or organisation that created it. It is down to you to assess the trustworthiness of a website – just as you would form an opinion about any person, company or organisation that you have dealings with. It's all about judgement and common sense.

I don't know how to assess a website though. What should I look for?

The main thing to consider is who runs it (there should be a contacts or 'about us' page that tells you this). If it is a reputable national body, such as a charity or government department, then the information is likely to have been rigorously checked. Commercial websites want to sell you something but some still have good information – they want to appeal to their customers and build a reputation for trustworthiness, after all. An individual's website or one that is loaded with advertising is much less likely to be reliable. And anonymous, unreferenced text – which has no named writer or organisation behind it – should be viewed with a sceptical eye. (There is more information about assessing information on page 170.)

Find what you want on the web

Search engines are a vital component of the web. They are designed to help you find the required needle of fact in a vast haystack of information. But to get the best from a search engine, you need to frame your query in terms that its computer brain can understand.

1. Start with word association. Search engines work by scanning the web for the words you type in. So think what combinations of words are likely to be on the page or in the answer that you're hoping to find. So, if you are looking for places to stay in Canada, the most direct and economical search would be 'hotel Canada' – or, better still, 'Hotel Quebec' or 'Hotel Toronto'.

2. Quote marks are a tool. If you put a phrase in double quotes when you search, the engine will seek out exactly that phrase in web pages. This can be useful if you are trying to find the author of a line of poetry (just type in the line, or part of it, inside double quotes) or if you want to find a statistic such as "population of the world in 1850". But don't put queries such as "How tall is the Eiffel tower" because you will exclude all the sites that don't include the question in that exact form of words. Better to type 'height Eiffel Tower', without quotes.

3. Say what you don't want. If you want to exclude a word from your search, type that word with a minus sign before it. Say you need a video of cats for a talk on feline behaviour, but when you type 'cats' all you get are cute 'out-takes' of cats falling off sideboards. Try searching on 'cats -funny'; that will weed out all the hits that are labelled as funny.

4. Say what's essential, too. If you put a plus sign before a word, this tells the search engine that this word must be present on all the pages it displays in the results. So 'four seasons +hotel' brings up search results that always have the words 'four seasons' associated with the hotel chain (rather than with the music of Vivaldi, the pizza or the times of the year).

5. Don't worry too much about spelling. Search engines usually offer you alternatives to the word you searched on if there is a more popular spelling. So if you type in 'elephonts', the search engine will recognise the misspelling and ask you if you meant to type 'elephants', with a clickable link that takes you straight to search results for 'elephants'. (But if you are in fact searching for, say, a rock band that's called Elephonts, then you can reject the search engine's prompt.)

6. Let the search engine itself answer your query. Some, such as Google and Ask.com, offer instant results, with no click-through needed. So you can type, say, 'convert 1 inch to cms' – and you'll be shown the answer straight away. Tap in 'capital Lithuania' and the word 'Vilnius' will pop up almost before you finish typing the keywords.

7. Search single websites. Type 'site:' then the simple name of the website (without the www.) directly after, with no space, then your search words. For example, 'site:msn.com berlin' brings up any pages on msn.com that have the word 'Berlin' on them.

8. Take your search to a higher level. All search engines have 'advanced options'. They are not advanced in the sense that you need special skills to use them. They are just a set of more sophisticated restrictions on the results that you get back. They allow you to choose to see results in particular languages or that originate in specified countries, among other things.

9. There's more than words. Most search engines look for text as a default, but they also allow you to search through images, videos, shopping products, maps, news and more. Have a look at what your search engine offers in the way of extra searches like this and try them out.

10. Don't be misunderstood. If, say, you were searching for information about breast cancer, it is possible that some explicit content might be among the results. But you can specifically filter out such material. On the Google home page, type in or click on **Preferences**, then tick the box under **SafeSearch Filters** that says **Filter explicit results.** On Bing, click the gear icon at the top right and under **SafeSearch** select the appropriate setting. In Yahoo!, perform a search and then to the right of the search box you'll see the **Options** menu. Click on this and select **Preferences** then in the **SafeSearch** section click **Edit** to tailor the options.

CUSTOMISE YOUR BROWSER

What should I use as my home page?

It can be good to stick with the default home page set by your browser – Chrome takes you to a tailored home page (called the New Tab page) that includes Google search as well as icons for the pages you use most often, for example. But if you want to change it, choose a site you often view – your favourite news page or a social media site such as Facebook. Alternatively, you may want to choose a search engine or webmail page.

How do I change my home page?

This is simple to do, but the method varies depending on the browser you are using.

In Internet Explorer

- Go to the web site you want. Click on the gear symbol ⚙ at the top right of the screen, then select **Internet Options** from the drop-down menu.

- A new window will appear. Select the **General** tab and under **Homepage** click on **Use Current**. The address of the page you are currently viewing should appear in the address box. Click **OK**.

In Chrome

- Go to the site you want and copy its web address in full (highlight the full address and click **Ctrl/Cmd+C**).

- Click on the three-lines symbol ☰ at the top right of the screen, then select **Settings** from the drop-down menu.

- A new window will appear. Under **Appearance**, where it says **Show Home button**, click on **Change** and then paste in the address of the site you copied. Click **OK**.

- If you want to change back to the New Tab page at any point, all you need to do is repeat the process but select the **Use the New Tab page** option instead of pasting in the web address.

In Safari and Firefox

- Go to the **Safari** or **Firefox** menu, then select **Preferences**. Select the **General** icon, then type in (or copy from the address bar) the web address you want into the **Homepage** bar.

Multitasking on a browser

Can I have more than one website open at a time?

It's very useful to keep one website open while you visit another, and all the commonly used browsers allow you to do this. It is like having a pile of books open on your desk: you don't have to close one and put it away before you move onto the next.

One way to open a second web page while keeping the first on screen is simply to open a new window (press **Ctrl+N**, or **Cmd+N** if you have a Mac). If you are on a PC and want to open a link in a new window, click with the right-hand mouse button; a pop-up menu appears, and you should choose **Open Link in New Window.**

I don't like having too many windows open at once, though.

This is where the tab function comes in handy. It allows you to see all the different pages that you have open – they are neatly displayed at the top of the screen, and look like those old-fashioned files that you used to find in a filing cabinet. All you need do to bring up the web page is click on the correct tab. You can even move tabs around by grabbing the tab you want to move (click and hold to do this), moving it to the position you want and then releasing the mouse button to drop it.

The easiest way to open a new tab is to click to the right of the existing one – depending on your browser, there may be a small + symbol here or a blank tab. Alternatively press **Ctrl/ Cmd+T**. Click the **X** button at the top right-hand corner to close the tab (Internet Explorer, Chrome, Firefox); if you are using Safari, the **X** is on the left.

Do tablets and phones use tabs?

They do. They may look exactly the same as on a computer. Or else you may see an icon consisting of two overlaying rectangles – like a couple of sheets of paper – at the bottom of the screen (this is how the Safari app on an iPhone works, for example). Tap this icon to see what pages you have open: the pages will come up in a kind of floating stack. You can bring a page to the fore by tapping on it, or close a page by tapping the X in the corner.

Your browsing history

I was on a great website, but can't remember what it was called. How can I find it again?

Your browser keeps a record of the sites that you have visited in the past days or weeks. This feature is known as History. You can use this function to keep an eye on what any children have been looking at on the web, although this is by no means definitive since it is easy to edit.

- In Internet Explorer 10, on the **View** menu, click **Explorer Bars** then **History**. (If you can't see the View menu, right-click in the blank area above your internet window and make sure **Menu Bar** is ticked.) Click on any of the dates listed on the left to open up a list of the websites you visited.

- In Safari, Firefox and Chrome, click on **History** from the menu at the top of your screen. In the drop-down menu that appears, you will see a list of the last websites that you visited. Click on any of these to view the website. Below this in Safari you will see the rest of the week's browsing history, organised into day folders; click on **Show All History** (Firefox) or **Show Full History** (Chrome) to view earlier history.

Can I change the length of time that my browsing history is stored?

It depends on the browser that you are using.

- In Internet Explorer 10, click on the gear icon, then select **Internet options** from the drop-down menu, then the **General** tab in the window that appears. Next click on **Settings** and tailor them to your needs.

- In Safari, go to the **Safari** menu, then select **Preferences**. Click on **General** in the window that appears. Change **Remove history items** to your preferred time period using the pop-up menu.

- In Firefox and Chrome, the browser itself determines how many pages can be kept – so you can only choose between remembering the history or disabling it altogether (find out how to disable your history opposite).

What if I want to delete History? I have been shopping for gifts, and I don't want to leave any clues!

Many people want to keep their browsing history private for a variety of reasons. It is very easy to do:

- In Internet Explorer 10, click on the gear icon, then **Internet options** from the drop-down menu, then the **General** tab in the window that appears. Under **Browsing History** click **Delete**, then select what you wish to remove and click **Delete** again.

- In Safari, go to the **History** menu. At the bottom of the drop-down menu you will see **Clear History**. Click on this to remove the record of the websites you have visited.

- In Chrome, click on the three-lines icon, select **History** and click **Clear Browsing History**, select the time period you require and then click on **Clear browsing data**.

- In Firefox, go to the **History** menu and select **Clear Recent History**. Choose the required time range from the window that pops up, and click **Clear Now**.

I don't like the idea of History being stored at all. Can I prevent this?

Many people are concerned about privacy and tracking on the internet, and want to browse anonymously. It's perfectly reasonable to want to do this, and browsers have made it easier for you:

- In Internet Explorer 10, click to open a new tab and select **InPrivate Browsing** from the new tab screen.

- In Safari, go to the main Safari menu and select **Private Browsing**.

- In Chrome, click on the three-lines icon and select **New Incognito Window** from the menu, or press **Ctrl/Cmd+shift+N**.

- In Firefox, go to the **Tools** menu and select **Start Private Browsing**.

If you browse anonymously, your browser will not keep a record of any websites you visit. Similarly, any files you download (copy) onto your computer will not be recorded in your download history.

Is my search engine keeping track of the websites I visit then?

Well, yes, it probably is. Any searches made from the same computer are tracked and kept by search engines for a fixed period of time. They can also be viewed by your ISP. That information is then analysed statistically, along with everyone else's searches, to give search engines an idea of what people want to know from them. Tracking also helps to spot fraudulent or criminal activity. Some search engines make a point of not storing any user details, and these include DuckDuckGo; you can also choose to search anonymously (see page 65).

Favorites and other useful features

There are some websites I use a lot. How can I remember what they are?

You are bound to have websites that you visit frequently. All browsers have a function that lets you list the websites that you visit most often; these can then be loaded quickly, without having to type in the address. In Internet Explorer this feature is called **Favorites**; in Safari, Chrome and Firefox it's **Bookmarks**. It is extremely useful and you may find yourself gathering a large, eclectic lot of bookmarks quite quickly.

A word of advice: keep them current by regularly deleting the ones that you no longer use, or organise them into folders from the start – otherwise you'll end up with an unwieldy list of websites.

How do I use Favorites or Bookmarks?

You need to be viewing a website in order to add it to your Favorites or Bookmarks. So type in the URL to get there. Then:

In Internet Explorer

• Click on the little star icon ★ at the top right of the browser window and select **Add to favorites**; a small window appears with the name of the web page – edit this to a shorter and more recognisable name.

• Create a new folder by clicking the **New folder** button next to it (choose a name that will make sense to you later – News Sites, say). Alternatively, click the **Create in box** to put the website into a folder you have set up previously. Click on **Add** once you have chosen the right place.

• To load one of your Favorites, simply click the star icon. You'll see a list of saved web pages and folders. Click on a folder to open it, then click on the web page you want to visit.

In Chrome

• Click on the star icon ★ at the far right of the address bar and a small Bookmarks box opens. Here you can change the name of the web page to something recognisable. Then click the arrow in the **Folder** area to bring up a list of folders; select the one you want to store the page in. Or select **Choose another folder** and click on **New folder** to create one.

• To load a website stored in your Bookmarks, click on **Other bookmarks** at the top right of the screen to bring up a list of folders; select the one you want by clicking on it, then click on the required web page.

In Firefox

• Click on the star icon ★ at the right side of the address bar; in the small box that pops up you can change the name of the web page. Click the menu next to **Folder** to bring up a list of folders. Select the one you want. To create a new folder, click on **Choose**, then click the + symbol. Give the new folder a name, and click **Done**.

• To go to a site stored in your Bookmarks, click on the star image at the top of the screen and select **Show All Bookmarks**. Click through to the right web page.

In Safari

• Click the + symbol on the toolbar; in the box that appears you can edit the name of the web page. Click on the arrow button to bring up a list of folders, select the one you want to store the page in and click **Add**. Create new folders using the **Bookmarks** menu at the very top of your screen.

• To view your bookmarked page, click on the book symbol on your toolbar, and click on the right folder, then the page you want.

How to speed up your browser

If your browser seems sluggish, there are some things you can do to get it working faster:

1. Time for a spring clean. Clear your browsing history by deleting your browser's history files (see page 65). Internet browsers store information about each website you visit. After a while, that data can begin to slow down the speed at which pages load.

2. Clean out your cache. Empty your browser's cache of temporary internet files – this is a folder on your hard drive where websites you have visited are stored by your browser to help speed up the time it takes to load the pages if you go back to them. There's no need to clear them out regularly (unless you want to for privacy reasons). But it's worth doing this from time to time because if it is full to bursting it will have the opposite to its intended effect and will slow your browser down. To do this in Chrome, click on the three-lines icon, and then **Tools**, **Clear browsing data**, select **Empty the cache** and choose the time period, then click on **Clear browsing data**. In Firefox, click on **Firefox**, **Advanced** then **Network**. Here you'll see exactly how large your cache is and have the opportunity to delete it. In Internet Explorer click on the gear icon, then **Safety**, then **Delete browsing history** and tick the option marked **Temporary Internet files and website files**, then click **Delete** (make sure nothing else on that list is ticked, or you'll delete that as well). Safari users should click **Safari**, then **Empty cache.**

3. Close the tabs. Tabs are a great feature as you can keep several web pages open at once and flick between them. If you find that your browser is slow and you have a lot of tabs open, close some of them and see if the speed improves (save them as bookmarks if needed). Each tab takes up memory on your computer and is therefore slowing you down.

4. Rationalise your add-ons. Each add-on takes up space on your computer, so don't keep them unless they are useful (see page 72 to find out about add-ons). To view your add-ons and delete any you don't need, in Chrome go to **Tools** then **Extensions**, in Internet Explorer go to **Tools** then **Manage add-ons**, in Firefox click **Firefox** then **Add-ons** and in Safari go to **Help** then **Installed Plug-ins**.

5. If you've tried all these fixes and your browser is still slow, consider switching to a different browser. Safari and Chrome are said to be fast browsers, possibly because they have fewer added extras than some other browsers. And consider upgrading your internet speed with your ISP, as this may help enormously.

What about if I am on my smartphone?

Tablets and smartphones allow you to make Bookmarks or Favorites into folders too. Go to your browser, and find Bookmarks or Favorites (a book or star icon). Click on **Edit** (on some phones this may be a pencil icon), and you should have the option to save to existing folders or to make a new one. On some phones, you can also save a web page to your home screen where it will look like yet another app – this way, you can visit it with one tap.

There are some websites that I visit every time I go online. Is there a quicker way of loading these?

One of these top sites should be your home page, of course. But most browsers allow you to save web pages to the Favorites/Bookmarks toolbar, which is along the top of your screen. This means you can open the web page with a single click. You'll find an option to place a website on the toolbar when you are saving it as a Favorite or Bookmark.

I can't see my Favorites/Bookmarks toolbar. How do I find it?

If the bar isn't visible:

- In Internet Explorer, right-click on the blank toolbar area at the top of the screen and select **Favorites bar** – it should then have a checkmark next to it. (Repeat to remove the checkmark and hide the **Favorites bar**.)
- In Safari, go to **View** and click on **Show Bookmarks** bar.
- In Chrome in Windows, click on the three-lines symbol, select **Bookmarks** and then make sure there's a tick next to **Show bookmarks bar**. On a Mac, go to **View** and select **Always Show Bookmarks Bar**.
- In Firefox, click on the star icon, and select **View Bookmarks Toolbar**.

I have loads of Favorites, but I haven't organised them. Help!

You can organise your saved web pages at any point – though it is a dull task. In Internet Explorer, click on the Favorites star icon at the top right of your browser window, then click the arrow next to **Add to favorites**. Now click **Organize favorites**. The box that appears contains a list of your Favorites. You can create new folders (click **New folder**, name it, then press **Enter**), click on links and drag them into folders, reposition your folders by clicking and dragging, and rename saved web pages or folders (click on the one you want to change, click on **Rename** and press **Enter**). To delete a saved web page or folder, click on it and then click **Delete**. Once you are happy with your reorganisation, click **Close**.

One handy tip if you can't face doing this: alphabetise! All you need to do is right-click on any item, and then click **Sort by Name**.

How do I arrange my Bookmarks?

It's a simple process but varies depending on the browser you are using:

- In Chrome, you can sort your Bookmarks by clicking on the three-lines icon, then on **Bookmarks**, then on **Bookmark Manager**. If you wish to order the links alphabetically, click on **Organize** and then **Reorder by title**. From that same **Organize** menu you can also click to add a new folder or new page. To move pages into folders, drag and drop them across the screen to the required folder.

- In Safari, on the **Bookmarks** bar click the open-book icon to open your bookmarks list. To add a new folder, click the + button at the bottom of the list on the sidebar at the left and type the name you want to give the folder. You can click and drag if you want to move them to a different place.

- In Firefox, click the star icon at the top right and choose **Show All Bookmarks**. A box with your bookmarks in it will pop up. If you want to alphabetise the links in any folder, right-click on that folder and select **Sort By Name** (or click and select this option in the three-lines menu). You can also move links and folders around by dragging and dropping them to the desired location on screen. If you right-click on any folder, you can choose **New Folder** to create a new folder right there (on a Mac, click on the gear icon and select **New folder** from there).

I am always spotting articles online that I want to keep for later. Is there a way of saving web pages temporarily?

Yes, there is. In Safari, this feature is built in. It's called Reading List, and the icon is a pair of spectacles. You click on this and a window appears to the left of the browser. Click on **Add** to save the web page, and you can read it offline. You can look at your reading list at any time by selecting **Show Reading List** in the **View** menu at the top of the screen. Delete an item by passing your mouse over and clicking on the **X** to the right; or select **Clear All**. Other browsers also have a Reading List function, but it is an add-on. It's called Read Later Fast in Chrome, and Read It Later in Firefox and Internet Explorer.

What exactly is an add-on?

It is an optional extra that you can add to your browser. Add-ons, extensions or plug-ins are software programs that add something to the website you are using and allow it to perform other functions. The Readability feature mentioned on page 56 is an add-on. Few of them are essential – but many are useful, or might fit your particular needs (there are add-ons that allow you to use diacritic marks in foreign language text, for example). A browser add-on could be, say, a video player that allows you to watch movies on a website. If you don't have the add-on required for that site, you won't be able to make use of all the functions the site offers – for example, you would just see text and wouldn't be able to view videos.

How do I know what extras I need?

If you need a video player, say, then your browser will bring up a message across the top of the internet page, saying that a certain add-on (or plug-in) is required and asking you if you wish to install it. If you feel you need the add-on to get the full benefit of the page you are viewing, then follow the instructions and download it (only if you trust the source, of course). Or find your browser's online store at iegallery.com, chrome.google.com, addons.mozilla.org, and extensions.apple.com and see what is available. But don't install add-ons unless you need them – they take up memory on your computer and may make your internet experience slower.

Downloading, saving, printing

What is downloading?

Downloading means copying a file from the internet onto your computer. The process is easy:

1. Find the file you want – it may be on an official website that you trust or in your browser's online store.

2. Click on the **Download** button.

3. Wait for the transfer to complete (you may be asked where you want to save the file first).

4. Find the file on your computer and double-click to open it.

5. When it opens, follow any set-up instructions.

If you are worried whether the add-on is safe or not to download, remember that up-to-date antivirus software will warn you not to download anything that is suspicious.

How do I save a web page?

In the same way as you save any document. Go to the **File** menu, and select **Save As** (or **Save Page As** on some browsers), then choose a location on your computer to save it to.

Can I save just the text?

Yes, you can. Some browsers allow you to save a text-only version when you do **Save As**. Alternatively, select the text you want to copy by using your mouse to highlight it. Then press **Ctrl/Cmd+C** to copy the text. Open word-processing software such as Microsoft Word and press **Ctrl/Cmd+V** to paste the text into a new document, then save that document wherever you want on your computer. You will probably need to change the font and size. Any links in the text will be preserved (so long as your word-processing software supports this) – if you click on them later, you'll be taken straight to the relevant website. Saving just the text will be easier if you are viewing the page in Reader or Readability (see page 56).

You can keep images on your computer but remember that most are subject to copyright and can't be used for professional or commercial purposes.

What about pictures – can I save those?

Yes, of course. If you are on a PC, you simply right-click on the image you want and select **Save image as** (or **Save picture as**). A window will then open; within this you can choose which existing folder you want to store the image in – or you can create a new folder to put it in. Give the image a name and click on **Save**. If you are on a Mac, simply click on the image and drag it onto your desktop. You can keep images on your computer but remember that most are subject to copyright and can't be used for professional or commercial purposes.

I want to print a web page. How do I do that?

A quick way to print a page in all browsers is to press **Ctrl/Cmd+P**. Alternatively, in Safari choose **File** then **Print**. In Chrome, click the three-lines icon and select **Print**. In Internet Explorer, click the gear icon and select **Print**, then click **Print** again on the new menu that opens. In Firefox, click the **Firefox** menu and select **Print**.

Up pops a print box with a menu of print options that you can adjust. Once you're happy with the options, make sure your printer is connected and switched on and click **Print** or **OK**. To close the print box, if you change your mind, click **Cancel**.

Sometimes a website will have a print button on the page, perhaps as an image of a page or a printer. If you click on this, a printer-friendly version of the page will load, so you'll have a better result when you print, with the text aligned properly and no spurious items such as menu lists and advertisements.

SAFE BROWSING

Why do some websites ask me to create a username and password?

Shopping websites, webmail and banks are among the sites that require you to have a personal account. This is so that you alone can view your own information and spend your money. Other sites, such as social networks, also need to know that you are who you claim to be.

What happens if I forget my password?

Don't worry if the 'memorable' password you chose does slip your mind. As well as setting a password, you may be asked to provide answers to some personal questions that enable the account to verify your identity if you forget your password. Answering a series of simple questions correctly, such as the name of your first pet, will allow your account access to be restored. (For extra security, it is a good idea to choose answers that aren't actually true – perhaps use the name of a friend's pet instead of your own if you think you can remember it.) After establishing that you are who you claim to be, some email providers may ask you to reset your password. Others may send you a verification code by text message on the contact number you provided when first setting up your account – you will be asked to enter it on screen before your account access is restored.

I heard pop-ups can be dangerous, but I am not sure what they are.

A pop-up is, as the name suggests, a window that pops up unbidden on your screen. It's okay if you know it's a safe pop-up – for example, a download you have requested from a reliable website. However, there are other pop-ups that open up when you visit certain websites, without you requesting them to do so. These are usually advertisements and could be from safe or suspicious sources. The pop-ups themselves are safe, it's the content in them that, if clicked, may not be. But they are annoying because they clutter up your screen, and stop you viewing the website you are on.

Password protected

It is not safe to use the same password for different accounts. You need to create lots of strong passwords, and to change them often. Here are some key pointers.

1. Avoid the obvious such as the word 'password', number sequences such as 123456, family or pet names, birthdays or anniversaries and your phone number. Avoid words that can be found in the dictionary, which hackers can easily guess.

2. Longer is stronger so make your password eight characters or more.

3. Use a collection of letters, numbers and punctuation marks or symbols – if you want to use pandabear56, for example, try pañdåbr56. Include upper- and lower-case letters if the site allows this.

4. Better still, use poetry. It's easier to remember a phrase than a random assemblage of characters. Take the first letter of each word from the lines of a favourite song or poem – for example, *Kubla Khan* by Samuel Taylor Coleridge starts: *In Xanadu did Kubla Khan/A stately pleasure-dome decree*. This produces an unguessable password that reads IXdKKAsp-dd. Change your poem often.

5. Use different passwords for important accounts (such as your bank or online stores). For less important accounts, you could append a suffix – such as fb (for Facebook) or tw (for Twitter) – to the same 'poetry' password.

6. If you can't remember your passwords write them down using some kind of code (try meaningful word associations that only you will understand). Don't make a file labelled 'Passwords' on your computer!

7. Use an online password manager to generate passwords and keep them safe for you. Try LastPass (lastpass.com), Roboform (roboformcom) or KeePass (keepass.info). Then all you need to do is remember one master password for the site.

What can I do to stop pop-ups?

Most browsers have a pop-up blocker that's turned on automatically and this stops all pop-ups from opening. If you're unsure, you can check the settings. In Internet Explorer, click the **Tools** menu then select **Pop-up Blocker** and make sure it is turned on. In Chrome, load the **Settings** menu via the three-lines icon, and click on **Show advanced settings**. Under **Privacy**, click on **Content Settings** and scroll down to find the pop-ups section and alter the settings. In Firefox, click the **Firefox** button then **Options**. Under **Content**, check that there's a tick next to **Block pop-up windows**. In Safari go to **Safari** then **Preferences** and click **Security**. In that section, click **Block pop-up windows**.

Is there anything else I need to be aware of when browsing?

If you're visiting European websites, you're likely to come across a banner message (across the top or bottom of the screen) about cookies when you visit new sites. This informs you that the site uses cookies and asks for your consent for cookies to be used (or not) while you browse.

Most browsers have a pop-up blocker that is turned on automatically and this stops all pop-ups from opening.

What are cookies?

Cookies are small files that websites install on your computer – generally for legitimate reasons. It is thanks to cookies, for example, that online shops recognise you when you visit ('Hello David, welcome back!'), saving you the trouble of logging on every time. In other words, websites use cookies to track your activity. When you load a site, your computer checks whether you have been there before and sends the cookie information to the site. The site may change the information it displays to you, so that you see something new. Some cookies track the time you spend on web pages, what you put in your shopping cart and more. All of this can contribute to a more tailored experience.

Is it okay to have cookies on my computer, then?

Usually, they are a convenience to you and will enhance your experience of any website where you spend money, share personal information (such as social networks) or otherwise have customised the page to suit your needs. So, it's not advisable to delete your cookies.

It is thanks to cookies that online shops recognise you when you visit, saving you the trouble of logging on every time.

I have noticed that I often see ads for things I have searched for online – is this connected to cookies?

This is called targeted advertising. Cookies can be used to build up a profile of you – based on what you do online. This information may then trigger personalised advertisements. It can be disconcerting to search for a watch, say, and then find an ad for this on your screen. But in a sense it is no different from what a supermarket does when you use a loyalty card.

I don't like it. How can I stop it?

Here are two things you can do to help stop targeted advertising.

- Browsers can send a 'Do not track' request to the websites that you visit. You will need to turn on this option in your browser settings. Be aware, however, that this is a request for websites not to track your browsing, rather than a guarantee that they won't.

- It's more effective to install an add-on that blocks advertising – the most popular is Adblock, which you can install from your browser's extensions store, or from adblockplus.org. This will stop targeted and other ads from being displayed on the websites you visit.

What about deleting the cookies?

You can certainly delete cookies if you think the downsides outweigh the benefits. To do this:

- In Chrome click on the three-lines icon, then **Settings** then **Show advanced settings** and under **Privacy** click **Clear browsing data** and select the option to **Delete cookies and other site and plug-in data** and click **Clear browsing data.**

- To remove cookies in Firefox, click on **Firefox**, **History**, then **Clear Recent History**. From here you can set the time range to, e.g. **Clear Everything** and tick **Cookies** on the list (and nothing else) then click on **Clear Now**.

- In Internet Explorer 10, click on the **Tools** menu and select **Delete browsing history** then tick the box next to **Cookies** and select **Delete**.

- In Safari, go to **Safari**, **Preferences** and then select the **Privacy** tab. Click on **Details** under Cookies to see a list of all cookies. You can either click **Remove All** or select individual cookies from the list to delete.

So, as long as I have antivirus software, is it safe to download from the web?

If you try to download anything that could be malicious software then your antivirus will flash up a warning and you should not proceed with the download. Remember you must keep your antivirus updated to be sure it offers the best protection. But you should always take notice of the source of the download – is it a site you can trust? If not then avoid downloading anything from it. If you didn't click on anything to make the download box appear, then the site is trying to make you download a file to your computer. This is another clue that it may not be safe or necessary.

What about my children – how can I make sure they are browsing safely?

There is plenty of safe, educational and fun content available on the internet for children. But it is essential to take steps to protect your children's safety when they browse the web – the web is designed for all ages and there is a lot of inappropriate content that can be viewed, whether intentionally or not. Both Windows PCs and Macs have parental controls that you can use to set time limits on computer use and restrict access to certain types of website.

How do I set these controls?

In Windows, go to the Control Panel and select **User Accounts and Family Safety**, then choose **Set Up Parental Controls For Any User.** On a Mac, open **System Preferences in the Apple menu**, select **Parental Controls** and follow the on-screen instructions. You can also set parental controls on most browsers to help protect children from offensive language, nudity, sex and violence.

Where do I find parental controls on my browser?

In Internet Explorer 10, click on the gear icon, then **Internet options**, then the **Content** tab and click on **Family Safety** and follow the instructions to set up an account for a child and to set the restrictions on what they can and can't see when browsing. If you use Safari, then you can also create a guest account for your child and enable parental controls – go to **System Preferences** in the Apple menu and choose **Accounts** to do this. Chrome allows you to create a 'supervised user' account for your child: you can allow certain websites and block others, as well as check what sites they have visited. Log in to Chrome, click on **Settings** in the three-lines menu and choose **Add new user** under **Users**. Firefox has something called FoxFilter that you can download from its online add-on store (see page 72). It allows you to block particular websites as well as any that contain inappropriate keywords. And if your child has a tablet or phone, you can install a parental controls app from the built-in app store.

Is there anything else I should do?

It's unwise to rely solely on parental controls. The best way to protect your children is to talk to them and make them aware of how to stay safe online – an open conversation with a caring adult is the most effective tool for keeping them safe. It is also important to monitor their browsing: you need to know when they are online and what they are doing. Keep the computer in a living area, and position it so that you can see the screen as you go about your daily business. Make it a rule that mobile devices are not used in bedrooms, out of sight. Use the History function to check what websites your child is using (bearing in mind that this can easily be disabled). And insist that you know the passwords for sites they have joined, so that you can check their activity from time to time.

Six top tips for internet safety

We have compared the internet to a big city full of attractions and diversions. But like a big city, the internet has its dark byways and risky neighbourhoods. You need to know how to skirt round them – especially if there are young people in your household.

1. If you use a public computer to log onto webmail, a shopping site, or any website that requires you to log in, make absolutely certain that you log out again once you have finished; don't just close the window. Staying logged in is like leaving your front door ajar: someone could happen by and gain access.

2. If for whatever reason you stop using an online bank account, or an internet shop, or a social media site, then close your account. Don't let it sit there dormant: though it's unlikely to happen, someone could get to it and exploit it.

3. If you have teenagers in your house, tell them to take care over what they post on social networks. Say: would you be happy for me, or a teacher or your grandmother to see what you are saying? If not, then don't post it. The same goes for you: avoid getting into online arguments (flame wars, as they are known) on social media sites.

4. Don't share identifying information with people that you only know online. And never use your name, home town or age in your usernames.

5. Don't give anyone else access to your online accounts or passwords. Make sure that all your accounts are protected by strong passwords (see page 76).

6. Impress upon any young people in your household that they should never, ever arrange to meet people that they have only been in contact with on the web. If you or anyone in your household does internet dating, then use a recommended, well-established company; and when you go on a date, make sure that you meet in a public place, that someone knows when and where it is taking place, and the name of the person you are meeting.

3

KEEP IN TOUCH

Starting points

- **If email were all the internet offered,** it would still be a wonderful invention. Email has revolutionised the way we keep in touch with each other.
- **Email is immediate and it's free** – more than **2 billion people** use it for business or to contact friends and family.
- **You can send photographs and documents** over the internet by attaching them to emails. You can send very large files by signing up to specialist websites.
- **The latest technology** means that you can make free phone calls – including video calls – over the internet.

KEY ACTIONS

- Set up a personal email account.
- Send photographs or documents with your message.
- Organise your inbox and keep track of your correspondence.
- Make an online contacts book to keep all your email addresses.
- Spot spam emails and stop them coming through.
- Catch up with friends and family through Skype, Facetime and instant messaging.

GETTING AN EMAIL ACCOUNT

What is email?

Email is short for 'electronic mail'. It's a way of sending written letters or messages across the internet – anything from a quick hello to a 100-page contract. When you send an email to someone, it arrives almost instantly, and sits waiting in an 'inbox' until he or she comes to read it. With email there is a facility for adding pictures or other digital files to the message – such as popping a photograph in the envelope when you send a letter, or posting a book or videotape or a formal invitation.

I want to use email. What do I need to do?

Before you can start sending emails, you'll need an email address, which will be unique to you. To get this, you'll need to sign up for an account with an email provider. In the first instance, your email provider will be the same company as provides your internet access (your ISP, see page 19) – an ISP will usually provide its customers with an email address when they sign up for its services. You can change this to something more personal or user-friendly, and the ISP will also allow you to set up more email accounts with different addresses – all as part of your internet package. There are other ways of getting an email address too (see page 88) – and many people have more than one (for example, one for work and one for home use, in the same way that someone can use two postal addresses: where they live and where they work.

How do I change the email address I have been given?

This varies from ISP to ISP, but generally you go to the company's own website and sign in, using the email address allocated to you. There you will find a link called something like **Manage your account**. Click on it, and you will be guided through the process.

Where do I send and receive my emails?

You either go online or you can use the software (called an email client) that is pre-loaded on your computer. Microsoft Outlook, Outlook Express and Entourage are the most commonly used email clients.

What is an email client?

The term 'email client' is a bit unhelpful: it is simply a program installed on your computer that allows you to compose and read emails offline (that is, when you are not connected to the internet) as well as to send and receive them. These programs were developed at a time when people were charged by the minute each time they went online. It therefore made sense to write emails in advance and then jump online to send them, and grab any new emails from your inbox as quickly as possible, before going offline again.

These days, now that broadband is widespread, most people's computers are constantly connected to the internet, so you don't necessarily need an email client. Lots of people prefer these programs because they find them easier for composing drafts of emails, maintaining lists of contacts, and organising and filing emails that they have sent and received. But using an email client is no longer the only sensible way to do email. Some people find it more convenient to use 'webmail' or use a combination of webmail and an email client.

And what is webmail?

Webmail is an email account that is accessed through an online website. You visit the site to read your email, and also to write and send emails of your own. This means that you need to be connected, of course (if your internet has gone down, then you cannot access webmail), but the convenience of this is that all your emails remain in the same place and they don't take up space on your computer.

How do I sign up to webmail?

You can usually access your emails through your ISP's website. And there are various free webmail accounts available too. The most popular include Gmail (the Google mail service), Outlook.com (which used to be known as Hotmail, and is owned by Microsoft) and Yahoo! Mail. They all work in the same way, allowing you to send and receive emails, to organise messages in your inbox into folders and to set up filters to stop you being bombarded by tiresome junk mails. All you need do is to go to the website, click on the option **Sign up** and give a few personal details, such as your name, date of birth and gender. You will then choose your email address and password.

I am hopeless at remembering passwords, though.

Most people have trouble keeping track of their passwords. You may be tempted to use the same password for everything (again, lots of people do) but this is unwise: you need a different lock for every door of your internet presence. It is often said that you should not write down your passwords. But actually this is a low-risk way of keeping track of them – especially if you take the extra precaution of, say, tucking the sheet of paper into a particular book on your shelves (just don't forget which book!). A more hi-tech solution is to register with an online password manager (see page 76). In short, it is not hard to keep hold of your passwords – including the ones that give you access to your various email accounts. (See page 75 for some guidance on what to do when a password has gone completely out of your head.)

So I can have several email accounts?

Lots of people do. It's useful to have separate email addresses for professional and personal purposes so it's easier to keep track of all your messages and contacts. And it is a good idea to have a 'spare' email address – ideally a webmail one – that you use to sign up for offers and newsletters online: this helps to limit the amount of marketing emails that come to your main email address. There's no limit to the number of accounts you can set up – you just need to keep track of the log-in details for each one.

Anatomy of an email address

Email addresses are similar to postal addresses, in that they are structured in such a way that your mail will be delivered to you – and only to you.

Every email address is essentially made up of two parts: the bit before the @ (which is the username) and the bit that follows it (the 'domain' name).

The username part is unique to you. In the same way that your specific house number identifies your home in your postal address, the local part of an email address allows your ISP to route the message to the correct mailbox.

The second, domain part might be issued by your ISP (internet service provider), your webmail provider or the company you work for; it is likely to be shared by many other users. Anyone can set up their own personal domain name, and you may decide to do this yourself – see page 92. The domain name is similar to the street or city name in a postal address, as it narrows down the destination that the message needs to be routed to. It includes the suffix, which is an indication (though not a guarantee) of what type of organisation owns the site and where it is in the world.

How do I choose an email address for myself?

Take a look at the box above to see how email addresses are constructed. The part that you can choose is the phrase before the @ sign: this is the username, which identifies you personally. So most people choose a version of their name, which has the advantage of being easy for other people to remember. Say your full name is Sarah Margaret Regan. You might opt for the username sarahregan, sregan, smregan or (though it's a bit on the long side) sarahmargaretregan. It is common to use punctuation such as full stops, hyphens and underscores to make a name more readable: sarah.regan, sarah-regan or sarah_regan.

Do I have to use my real name?

No, you can use any words you like. Choosing a facetious or witty name may seem like a good idea when you set up your email, but it may feel less hilarious when you have to confess 'I_love_pie' each time you want to pay a bill online. It may be sensible to stick to something straightforward, and express your personality by other means.

What if I have a common name... or else one that is hard for others to spell?

If your name's really popular, and you are using webmail or an ISP's domain name, then it is sure to have been snapped up for use already. The address john.smith@anywebmailaccount.com will undoubtedly have been taken. So try adding another element, such as a number or your middle initial (for example, john.m.smith or john.smith60). At the other end of the scale, if you have a long name or one that is hard to type or spell, you may want to simplify it – because all it takes is for one letter in the address to be spelled wrong, and your emails will not reach you. If you have a name such as Konstantin Gorodetzky, you could make an easily spelled acronym of it, or a short version: kongor, or gorod, say.

Choosing a facetious or witty name may seem like a good idea, but may feel less hilarious when you have to confess 'I_love_pie' every time you want to pay a bill online.

What about the bit of the address after the @ sign? Do I get to choose that?

Not usually. When you register for a personal email account, the part after the @ sign – the so-called domain name – usually consists of the company name of the email provider: yahoo.com or gmail.com, for example. Many people find that the domain name provided by their ISP or their webmail account meets their needs. However, businesses and professionals generally choose to register a name that is a version of the company's name, which they then use for their website and as the email domain for all employees. Some individuals choose to register their family name as a domain, and set up distinct and easy-to-remember email addresses for different family members – James Matthewson could in theory register 'Matthewson' as his personal domain, and set up individual accounts for himself, and his wife and son (james@matthewson.com.au, lucy@matthewson.com.au and ben@matthewson.com.au). One good reason for doing this is that your email address will stay the same if you change ISP.

That's a great idea. Can I pick any name I like?

You can if it is available. But the internet has been around for many years now, and so pretty much any common name has already been taken. You are more likely to have success with a made-up name or combination of two or more names or words: cowleyjones, juliamariafernandes.

How do I know what is available?

Domain name registration companies, such as 123-reg.com, can guide you through the process, including searching to see if your chosen name is available or already in use. You can't use anything offensive, libellous or copyrighted, and you need to steer clear of anything that is very similar to a known brand or famous person's name as this could embroil you in a legal challenge (it has happened more than once).

Know your email program

There are lots of different email programs, but they are broadly similar to each other. The design may vary, as may the names of some of the functions and the appearance of the icons. But they all allow you to carry out the full range of basic functions: sending and receiving email, organising messages into folders and deleting them, searching email for a particular message.

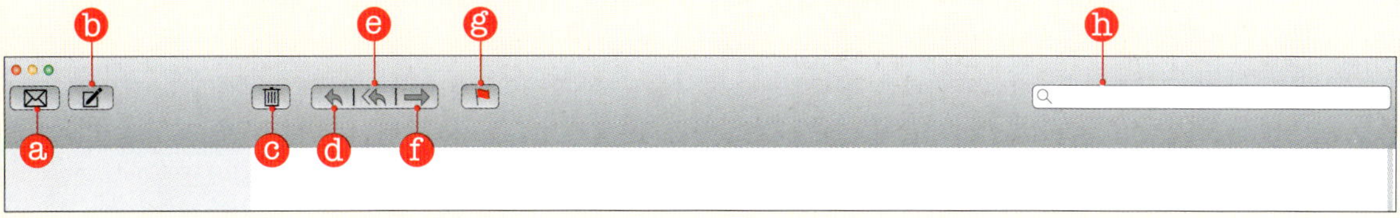

a Send and receive All programs have a button that you press to receive new emails and send ones that you have ready in your outbox folder. This may be an envelope, or an envelope with arrows round it.

b Compose Click on the compose icon – normally a sheet of paper and pencil – to create a new email for sending

c Delete Click on one or more emails to highlight them, then click on the rubbish bin or X icon to move them to the deleted items folder.

d Reply Open an email or click to highlight it, then press the reply or arrow icon. Write your answer in the space at the top; the original email and details of when and by whom it was sent are underneath.

e Reply All Click on this icon if you want to send a reply to everyone copied into the original email.

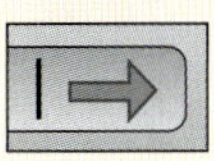

f Forward This allows you to send an email on to another recipient. As when you reply, the original email plus details of the sender will appear under your new email. You can edit the original email if you like.

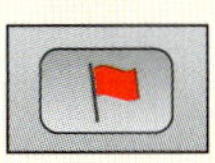

g Flag You can often flag important emails by clicking on a flag (or star) icon – useful if you get a lot of mails. It then appears next to the email in your inbox so you can spot it easily; you can search for flagged items, too.

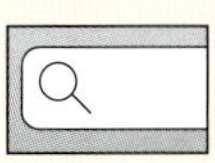

h Search bar Track down a particular email by entering a keyword here; it could be anywhere in the email from the sender's address to the text of the email itself. Some email clients allow you to search particular aspects of an email (sender, date, recipient) in an additional window.

Is it free to have your own domain?

No, you have to pay a small annual fee. Commercial organisations are obviously happy to pay this fee but private individuals may not feel that it is worth it, just for the fun of 'owning the rights' to their surname. The charge varies, as with any service provided by a commercial organisation. But think in terms of an annual fee that works out at the price of a few CDs.

I have my email address and want to set it up on the email client program on my computer. How do I go about it?

It'll take only a few minutes to get your email client set up and ready to receive and send emails. When you open the program for the first time, you will be prompted to create a new account. The exact instructions on how to do this will differ according to the client you are using and whether you're on a Windows PC, Mac or tablet. Look for the **Tools** drop-down menu and then select the **Accounts** menu. You'll need to enter some details, including your name, email address and password, and (in some cases) the type of server you want to use to access your email, selecting either IMAP or POP3 (see opposite).

It'll take only a few minutes to get your email client program set up and ready to receive and send emails.

What do IMAP and POP3 mean? And does it matter which one I choose?

IMAP is short for Internet Message Access Protocol and POP3 means Post Office Protocol version 3. Don't worry too much about remembering what these terms mean as you won't need to give them any more thought once you have gone through the initial account set-up process. They relate to the way in which messages sent to your email account are received and stored.

IMAP is the best option to choose if you regularly check your email from different devices, as POP3 emails may be deleted from the server once they have been delivered to your email client depending on how you set it up. This means that if you access your email from a mobile device, messages will be downloaded to that device and deleted from the server; they won't automatically appear the next time you sign in from your home computer. With IMAP, you download messages to your computer but they are synchronised with the master copy of your inbox folder, which is retained on the ISP's computer. This is useful if, say, your computer malfunctions as there will always be a retrievable copy of your correspondence. To find it, you sign in online, using your email address and password.

Is it the same for outgoing mail?

No, the server that sends emails from your account is called the SMTP server. This stands for Simple Mail Transfer Protocol. While you are setting up your account access in your email client program, you'll need to enter some additional details relating to your ISP here, but these will be provided by your ISP as a matter of course.

I have a tablet. How can I access my emails on it?

It's even easier to set up your email on a tablet (or a smartphone). It comes pre-loaded with an email app; it is often called Mail. The first time you press the icon ✉ – it is usually an envelope – you'll be asked if you want to set up a new account. Simply tap in your email address and the password, and give the account a name ('My email' will do). You can add another account at any stage by going into the general **Settings** menu and selecting **Mail** or **Accounts** and then **Add account**.

SENDING EMAILS

I want to write my first email.

Start by opening your email program, and clicking on the new email icon – often [icon] or the word **New**. Where you find it on your screen differs from program to program, but it's usually in a prominent place. A blank message template will launch. Pressing **Ctrl+N** on a PC (this is a useful keyboard shortcut) will also perform the same action; on a Mac, use **Cmd+N**.

The uppermost line is the To: line. This is where you enter the email address of your recipient. Be sure to enter the address correctly or it won't be possible for your email provider to deliver the message and it will be returned to you. Below this field, you'll also see a Subject: line and the main message body, which is where you type your message.

Email etiquette

Is an email a formal letter, or a casual chat in written form? Well, it depends who you are addressing, and what you are discussing – the key thing is to make your message clear and unambiguous. But there are some rules you should apply to all emails. Here are seven tips.

1. Get the tone right from the outset. Say you are writing to Mr Max Anderson, CEO of Acme Limited. If you have never met, or if there is a need to be deferential (say, you are asking him for a job), then start your mail 'Dear Mr Anderson'. If you and Mr Anderson are acquaintances or work colleagues, then 'Hi Max' is fine. Sign off with 'Best wishes' or 'Kind regards'.

2. Use the subject field. A blank subject field is unhelpful, so be sure to include one. The title of your mail should give the recipient an idea of the contents of your mail, and help them to relocate your mail three months down the line. So it is better to write 'Central heating breakdown – Stephen Evans', rather than something like 'I'M FREEZING HERE – PLEASE HELP!!!!'.

3. On that subject, avoid using capital letters or exclamation marks for emphasis – it's like shouting. Similarly, shortforms (gr8 for great, and so on) are not really appropriate in an email.

4. Acknowledge important emails if there is a chance that the sender will be anxious to know it has got through. You can be very brief: 'Hi Jenny, I received your mail and will get back to you later this week. Thank you. Ruby'.

5. Don't use email for secrets. Though you might have mailed someone in confidence, emails can be left open on a screen, get printed out or forwarded on. Think twice about writing anything you wouldn't say out loud and in public.

6. Never forward an email with a sarcastic comment attached. If you hit **Reply** by mistake, your sharp comment will end up in the hands of the person it refers to. Very embarrassing. Also, if you receive a group email and reply to one person on the list, make sure that you don't hit the **Reply All** button.

7. Don't send emails when you are annoyed. The instant nature of email means it is tempting to fire off a quick response – or to make a sarcastic comment – and then regret it. Put these emails in the drafts folder and re-read them before pressing the **Send** button.

Can I send an email to more than one person at the same time?

Yes, you can – type the email addresses of your intended recipients on the To: line, separated by a semi-colon, and send the email in the usual way (in some email programs, you click **Add** and enter each address in a different field). The message will be delivered to everyone at the same time.

Another way of sending an email to more than one person at the same time is by using the CC: field. This is usually located underneath the To: field. CC: is short for 'carbon copy' (a nod to the days of old-fashioned typewriters and carbon paper) and allows you to 'copy' other people in on an email you are sending without having to retype the whole email again. All other recipients will be able to see the email addresses of everyone else the email is being sent to.

Is there a way to send a message to a group of people without everyone being able to see who else it's going to?

Yes, there's a facility called BCC:, which stands for 'blind carbon copy'. By adding people's email addresses to this line, they will receive the same message as the people in the To: line, but none of the other recipients will be able to see anyone else's name or address – which would be a small but annoying breach of their privacy.

I've filled in all the boxes. What now?

Now you're ready to start typing your email in the main message window. If you prefer, you can also copy text you have typed in a word-processing program and paste it into the message field. When you have finished your message, simply press **Send**. The message will whizz off on its way through the superhighway to its destination inbox. You don't need to worry about physically typing your email address at the end of your message, as it will automatically be sent to your recipient. The message will also include the date and the time that your message was sent.

Can I read an email once I have sent it?

Yes, a copy will be stored in your sent items folder, and you can retrieve it from here if you want to. Also, if you want to write an email and revise or send it later, then click on **Save draft** or (if you are working in an email program installed on your computer) press **Ctrl/Cmd+S**. You will find it in your drafts folder.

How safe is webmail? Can other people get into my account and read my messages?

Your webmail account will be protected by a password. You'll be asked to enter this password each time you log in. This ensures that access to your inbox is granted only when the correct password is entered. To keep your account safe and secure, it's wise to make it as difficult as possible for others to guess – anyone who knows or guesses your password can get into your emails. Malicious software, such as viruses, may also target your email – another reason to have up-to-date antivirus software (see page 36).

Some webmail providers use software to scan emails that you receive (and send) for keywords; these trigger advertisements, which appear on your screen. So you may email a friend about the fact that you are thinking of buying a hatchback, only to find car advertisement pop up. Ads are a fact of many webmail accounts – it is one reason why they are free to use – but this is an automated process: nobody is actually reading your email to look for keywords. You can opt out of these targeted ads in some webmail accounts – look in your **Settings** menu to do this. You will still receive ads but they won't specifically relate to any information in your emails.

What about the emails that I send? Who can read those?

Once you have sent your email it can, of course, be read by anyone who has access to the recipient's account. It is also possible that an administrator at the company providing your email services could retrieve and read your email. This is very unlikely, but if you are sending highly confidential information (for example, you are emailing your bank), it is much safer to use an online enquiry form.

I'll often be emailing the same people. Do I have to type in their addresses every time?

No, you can save them as contacts in your email account, in the same way that you'd write their full postal address in an address book. You can add people to your **Contacts List** (or **Address Book**) by typing their email addresses in manually and saving them. Alternatively, once you've received an email in your inbox, you have the option of saving the sender to your **Contacts List**. This is more reliable, as it means their address will be stored accurately, whereas doing it manually allows you to enter and save a mistyped email address.

How do I use the address book?

When you compose a new email, you can select a recipient from your online address book, and his or her email address will be copied into the To: box. In an email program on your computer, you will see the **Address Book** button at the top of the new message screen, and by clicking on this, you can search for the address of any person you have saved as a contact.

Also, clicking on the To: box will bring up your full contact list in alphabetical order and you can search by typing in the first few letters of the person's name or scrolling down through the whole list. In many webmail programs, a list of the addresses you frequently send to will appear underneath the To: box – you simply click on the one you want.

All about attachments

How do I attach photos to an email?

Start composing your new email in the way described above, by clicking on **Compose** and entering your recipient's email address in the To: line. Next, click on the paperclip icon that is visible at the top level of the message screen. This enables you to include items (referred to as 'attachments') with your message.

A window appears showing the files on your computer and you'll be able to find a photo that you've saved on your hard drive or on an external USB flash drive (memory stick). Select the file you want to attach by clicking on its name. When you select **Open** (on a Windows PC) or **Choose** (on a Mac), the file you have selected will now be attached to your email. On a tablet, touch the paperclip icon and pick the picture you want from the **Choose Attachment** menu that pops up. Repeat this process if you want to add more than one photo to your message.

In some email programs you may also be able to drag files into the message body and they will be saved as attachments.

My photos are really large, and it's taking ages to add each one. Can I do anything to speed this up?

It's sensible to resize your images before attaching them. Photos taken on high-resolution cameras are big files, and this may mean that your message is too large for your email account to handle. Some email programs may automatically offer to resize images when sending images from a smartphone or tablet.

On a Mac

An option to resize image files is built into the Mail email program, so simply attach your photo, and look for the **Image Size** drop-down box at the lower right-hand corner of your message. There, you can choose between small, medium, large or actual size. If you are using another email account, then you will need to resize the image in the Preview application – click on the image, then go to **File** and select **Open With**, choosing **Preview** from the menu that appears. When the image appears, click on **Tools** and select **Adjust Size**. Change the width in the window that appears; the height should adjust automatically so long as the **Scale proportionally** box is ticked. The resulting size will be shown in the box below. Go to **File** again and click on **Save a version** or **Save as**, giving it a new name (you don't want to overwrite the original image with the smaller version). Then you should be able to attach it to your email.

On a Windows PC

The simplest way to resize your images is by opening your computer's photo-editing software and selecting the **Picture** or **Image Size**, **Resize** or **Resample** button. A box will open, where you can state the percentage of the original size that you'd like the photo to be resized to – choose a significantly smaller number. You'll need to save these smaller files as copies of the originals so you don't overwrite your high-quality photos, but now you'll be able to add them to your email without worrying about them being too large to be delivered.

Sending multiple or large files

If you attach a lot of files to an email, then it may not go through – and even if it does, it may then be rejected by the recipient's computer. This is because email programs are not designed to handle huge parcels of data. One solution is to combine the files into a folder and compress it. In Windows, right-click on the folder and select **Send to**, then choose **Compressed (zipped) folder** and a new folder will be created (it has the same name but the icon is slightly different, with a zip on it). On a Mac, click on the folder and then select **Compress file** in the **File** menu, and a new folder will be created. You will find the compressed folder in the same location as the original, and can then attach it to an email in the usual way (look for the .zip suffix on the filename to check it is the right one before you send it).

Very large files can be sent using a website specially designed for this purpose – Hightail, Dropbox, SendSpace or WeTransfer are four examples. These websites allow you to upload large files to the internet and simultaneously send a link via email to the recipient, who can then download them directly onto their computer via their browser.

Can documents and other files be sent in the same way?

Depending on the size of the file you want to send, the process is fairly similar. Again, some files may simply be too large to attach (see above for some alternative ways to send them). But word-processed documents or spreadsheets can be attached in the same way as photos, by clicking on the paperclip icon, locating where the file is stored on your computer and selecting the name of the file that you want to attach. Click **Open/Choose** and the file will be attached to your message.

I sent an email with a file attached, but it hasn't got there. What happened?

If you are sure that the email address is correct, it may be that the recipient's email provider has identified your email as junk – ask the recipient to check his or her junk mail folder. Or it may be that the file was too big to send. You should get a message in your inbox to tell you if an email hasn't arrived, but occasionally this doesn't appear or it goes into your junk mail.

When your recipient opens the mail, he or she can click directly on the link and be taken to the site you have chosen.

I want to include a link to a website in my email. How do I do that?

This is easy to do. Have the website open in a separate page in your browser. Highlight the website address in the address bar and press **Ctrl/Cmd+C** to copy it. Switch to your email message and press **Ctrl/Cmd+V** to paste in the address. In most email programs, the text is automatically turned into a clickable link: your recipient can click on this 'live' text and be taken straight to the relevant website. If you are on webmail, you can also click on the link icon – it looks like the link of a chain – in the menu of extras that appears above your message and a box appears for you to fill in the website address. In some email programs, you may also need to press the link icon (this may be in the **Insert** tab). Some email programs don't have this function at all and the person who receives the email will need to copy and paste the website address into his or her internet browser and open the link that way.

To check whether your link is working, save the email (by pressing **Ctrl/Cmd+S**) and then go to your drafts folder to find it – the link should now be blue and clickable.

RECEIVING EMAILS

How do I open and read emails that have been sent to me?

When you launch your email program, you'll be taken to a screen showing your inbox. All the messages you have received are listed here chronologically, with the ones received most recently at the top by default. (You can also choose to sort messages alphabetically by sender, by subject or in reverse chronological order, for example.)

At a glance, you will be able to see the name of the sender, the subject (so long as they have added one) and the date and time the message was sent. To open and read an email, simply click on the relevant line in your inbox and the full message will open. Some email programs automatically show you a message preview, which appears next to your inbox when you highlight a particular email, so you can quickly scan the contents of a message without actually opening it.

How do I know when I have been sent a new message?

When you visit your inbox, any new, unread messages will appear in bold type. A number also appears in brackets next to the inbox button telling you just how many new messages you have received since you last checked. Some email programs offer a new message alert facility which, if your computer is on, alerts you with a sound or pop-up box every time a new email arrives.

How do I reply to a message?

This is easy. By clicking on Reply (or the reply icon, which is often a left-pointing arrow symbol) you can reply to any message you've received. The original email you received will appear in the message body too, together with the information about when it was sent, who sent it and the message subject – this makes it easier for either you or the recipient to refer back to the previous message.

Type your message in the message body box, in the same way as if you were typing a brand new message, except the previous correspondence appears underneath your message. When you've finished, press **Send**. Your recipient will receive your reply in just the same way as any other email, except the email subject will be preceded by 'Re:' (e.g. you received an email with the subject 'Lunch today?', and the subject line of your reply will appear as 'Re: Lunch today?').

The original email was sent to a few of us. Can I reply to everyone at the same time?

If a message you receive has been sent to more than one person, you can choose to reply to the sender only as outlined above, or to all recipients. Select **Reply All**, or the keyboard shortcut **Ctrl/Cmd+Shift+R**.

I want to send the email on to someone else. Is that possible?

Yes, you can forward the message on to a new recipient, by clicking **Forward** (or **Ctrl/Cmd+F**) and typing their email address in the To: line. They will receive a copy of the email originally received by you. The original sender won't be aware that their message has been sent on to someone else (unless you accidentally hit **Reply** rather than **Forward**).

I've received a new email with a file attached. How do I open it?

First of all, be extra careful when receiving emails with files attached, and check that they are from a sender you recognise before you open any attachments. It's very common for spam messages to be sent with virus files attached – if you open them, they could 'infect' your computer and cause it to slow down or stop altogether, or they could destroy your files.

That's a worry. How do I know that an attachment is safe?

An attachment sent by someone you know and trust is a safer bet than one from a complete stranger. But occasionally you will get suspect emails from your contacts – if, say, their email account has been accessed by wrongdoers. If the message doesn't sound like the person you know – the tone just doesn't seem quite right, say – or is simply directing you to open the attachment, be very wary. If there seems anything odd about an attachment, then don't open it until you have confirmed that it is okay with the sender. (For more on this, see opposite.)

Email viruses

Email is one of the ways that computer viruses can spread. The damaging 'infection' can be hidden in an attachment. But you can guard against them if you know how to spot the tell-tale symptoms.

Computer viruses are so-called not only because they spread like a disease, but also because the infected file, once inside the host, reproduces itself like a biological virus, attaching copies of itself to programs and other files that are saved on your machine. This can drastically slow down the performance of your computer, and in extreme cases may mean you have to enlist professional help to get it up and running again. The species of virus known as spyware and Trojans also pose a massive security risk, as the infected files can allow hackers to tap into your machine and access any sensitive information it contains.

As with human viruses, you can reduce the risk of infection through some simple computer 'hygiene'. First of all, you need to ensure that your firewall is switched on and that you have antivirus software installed – see Chapter 1 for details about this. But you also need to be email-savvy

Here are five steps to avoiding viruses.

1. DELETE emails from unknown sources or unlikely addresses without opening them. An email address that reads joey786940754, for example, is probably a computer-generated spam account: it is not a name a human would pick.

2. DON'T OPEN attachments from unknown senders.

3. THINK before opening an attachment – even when it is from a known sender. Consider emailing the sender (in a separate email, not by hitting **Reply**) to check that it is genuine. Be wary, too, of attachments that have been compressed (these may end in .zip or .rar) since this is one way that spammers get round the filtering programs. Save them onto your computer and scan them using antivirus software before opening the files.

4. LOOK OUT for odd file formats, such as those ending .scr and .exe.

5. BE CAUTIOUS before clicking on links in emails – these may take you to a website that could attempt to download a virus onto your machine. Be especially wary if the email isn't personally addressed – an email that simply says 'Hey, have a look at my holiday photos' without a name is highly likely to be malicious.

I'm sure this attachment is okay. How do I open it?

When you're ready to open the attached file or photograph, open the email and then open the document icon 🗎 by clicking. If you are using webmail, you can usually choose to open the attachment on the web (click on **View Online** or **View as HTML**). Alternatively, you can transfer the attachment to your device and open it there – select the **Download** option to do this. On other email programs, you can save the open document to your hard drive (you can also drag the icon there).

Where does a downloaded file go?

When a file is downloaded onto your computer, it is usually saved to your hard drive if you are on a Windows PC and to a folder called Downloads on a Mac or tablet. You'll be able to view the files that have been saved by locating this folder and opening them there. On a Mac, the Downloads folder is usually present in the grey sidebar at the left of Finder windows. This means you can get to a downloaded file with one click.

ORGANISING YOUR EMAILS

I get lots of emails and want to be able to find particular ones without going through my entire inbox.

Filing your emails is a good habit to get into: you can set up your own subfolders and organise your messages in any way you choose. There are usually five existing folders in your email account (Inbox, Sent Items, Drafts, Junk/Spam and Deleted Items/Trash), which cannot be removed or renamed, but you can add your own subfolders to your inbox and group messages according to subject or sender.

How do I add my own subfolders?

It's easy to do this. Simply select Inbox in the list of folders. Then you can either right-click (on a Windows PC) and choose **New Folder**, or select the **File** tab from the menu at the top of your computer, and choose **New Folder** from the list of options. You'll be able to enter a name for your new folder and then click **OK** to save it. Your new subfolder will appear below the main inbox folder. You can then move messages to these new subfolders by clicking and dragging, or choose to have all correspondence from certain email addresses automatically delivered to a specific subfolder.

If you're using webmail the process to create and organise folders is essentially the same (although rather confusingly, Gmail calls folders 'Labels'). In the left-hand drop-down menu look for **New Folder/Create New Label** at the bottom of the list of options, give it a relevant name and once you've pressed **Enter** or **Create**, you'll see it has been added to the list of folders. Select any email in your main inbox that you'd like to move to this subfolder by pressing **Ctrl+Shift+V** (**Cmd+Shift+V** on a Mac) and choosing a new destination, or by highlighting the message you want to move and clicking on the **Move** button.

Should I delete old messages?

You don't have to if you are on webmail. There's no harm in keeping messages from contacts, and you may want to refer back to your emails later on. You may as well delete any junk mail or old emails that you no longer need, though. If you are using an email program installed on your computer, then you should clear out your inbox regularly since this reduces the amount of disk space being used, which can slow your computer down.

Email hoaxes and scams

Don't let the internet fraudsters and 'phishers' come angling for your usernames, passwords or credit card details.

There are some emails that you should view with deep suspicion. These include any mail that asks you to type in your password in order to have continued access to your bank account or other online payment site. It may look genuine – right down to the company logo – but in fact your bank would never ask you to do this. This is a scam known as 'phishing': the email is the bait and you are the catch. By clicking on the link and supplying the information requested, you are handing your details to fraudsters.

You might also receive an email telling you that you've won the UK lottery, or that you have inherited a small fortune from a millionaire relative you have never heard of, or that your help is needed to access a large sum of money, from which you get to keep a generous commission. You know what? It's a hoax, and the hoaxers are just hoping that you will be foolish enough to give them access to your bank account (so that the imaginary money can be transferred to your account straight away).

Here are three steps to avoiding the hoaxes.

1. DON'T PROVIDE personal or financial information to a website that you opened by clicking on a link in an email.

2. IGNORE emails from companies that you have never heard of.

3. NEVER GIVE your password, bank or other financial details or any private information to a website that you have accessed via an email link – it just isn't safe. Instead, type in the URL and log in as usual. Send a copy of the email to the company to alert them.

How do I delete messages that I no longer need?

Deleting messages is quick and easy. Select the email that you want to delete in your email list. In some programs, you will see a blank tickbox on the left, which you should click; otherwise, simply click on the message. Then click the **Delete** button or icon (which may look like a rubbish bin 🗑) and the message will instantly vanish from your inbox. (See 'I deleted a message by accident' below for where the message goes and how to get rid of it permanently).

I have lots of messages to delete. Is there a quick way to do this?

You can mark lots of messages for deletion if they have tickboxes – just select all the ones you want to remove one by one. To delete a consecutive run of messages, click on the uppermost message, then hold down the **Shift** key and click on the last one. This selects those messages and all the ones in between – clicking **Delete** moves them all to the Deleted Items folder. To delete every message from your inbox, press **Ctrl/Cmd+A** (a handy shortcut for 'Select All'), and click **Delete** – and you'll be looking at an empty inbox.

I deleted a message by accident. Can I get it back?

It's easy to get a message back if you have a change of heart. Deleted messages are not actually deleted straight away. They are merely moved to another folder called Deleted Items. If you decide that you actually do need to keep hold of the message, simply retrieve it from this folder by selecting the message you want, and either choose the **Move to Inbox** option (or similar) or drag it back into your inbox. If you are using a non-web-based email program, you should clear out your **Deleted Items** folder from time to time – simply select the items and then click on **Delete** – because they are still using up disk space all the time they are there. (Once you delete items from the Deleted Items folder, they really are gone and you can't get them back.) You don't have to bother with this if you use webmail, because deleted items are cleared out automatically, like a rubbish collection.

I'm looking for a particular message, but I can't remember when it was sent. Do I have to scroll through my whole inbox looking for it?

No, you can search your inbox or any subfolders for a specific keyword that is contained in the message, or for all messages from a certain sender. Click on the **Search** icon – a magnifying glass 🔍 – and enter your term in the box. All emails matching your search term will be displayed, hopefully allowing you to track down the item that you're looking for.

There are loads of emails with my search term. How can I narrow down the search?

When you click on the Search icon or box, you should get the option to do an **Advanced Search**. This allows you, for example, to specify the time frame when the email was sent (this can be as narrow or wide as you like – anything from a day to several years), to specify the sender, recipient or subject or whether or not it has an attachment. You can also search particular folders.

I've had my account for a few months now, and keep receiving emails asking me to buy products or services. How can I stop this?

These kind of messages are known as spam and are mainly harmless, although they do become rather annoying when they're flooding your inbox. If you have signed up for newsletters or alerts to special promotions that you no longer wish to receive, you can unsubscribe to these by clicking on a link in the email that you have been sent and ask for your name to be removed from their mailing list. But be very cautious about answering any emails from unknown senders – these are often spam emails, which are sent to thousands of likely email addresses.

Yes, I keep getting messages from companies I have never heard of. Can I stop these spam emails?

Those irritating advertising emails are a huge part of the whole 21st-century email experience. Research suggests that spam messages account for around 90% of all email sent. But email providers filter out as much as possible to reduce the amount in your inbox. Here are a few things you can do to help manage spam.

1. The default 'standard' (or 'low') filter is usually enough for most people, but you can usually increase the level of spam filters you have, block particular senders or even restrict your emails to known senders only. To do this, go to the settings menu: in webmail, this is often a gear icon ⚙ in the right-hand corner. If you have Outlook Express, you will find it in the **Home** tab, in the **Delete Group**; click **Junk** and then **Junk Email Options**. Other email programs may locate it in the **Tools** menu.

2. Report spam in a webmail inbox to the provider – you should get the option to block the sender (though often the spammers will use many different email accounts).

3. Check your junk mail folder regularly, to ensure that wanted emails aren't being misdirected there. You can move these emails to your inbox, and add the sender to your address book to prevent this happening again.

4. Some spam is bound to slip through the net – always delete or ignore it rather than respond. Never click the unsubscribe link in an unsolicited email – this just alerts the spammers to the fact your email address is active, and you may then notice a huge increase in the amount of spam messages you receive.

Delete email that looks like junk email without even opening them. And whatever you do, don't reply to spam messages.

FREE CALLS ON THE WEB

I've heard of Skype. What is it and how does it work?

Skype is a service that offers VoIP (which is short for Voice over Internet Protocol) to its subscribers. This technology allows you to use your computer to make calls to anyone in the world. Better yet, you can make video calls – a long-held dream of science-fiction writers – free of charge. You can also use Skype services to send text messages on your computer.

What do I need to make video calls?

If you have a webcam, you can use Skype to make free video calls to anyone else with a Skype account, as long as they have a webcam installed too. Simply work out a mutually convenient time across the different time zones, and within a matter of seconds, you could be having the next best thing to a face-to-face chat with relatives thousands of kilometres away.

If you don't have a webcam, Skype also lets you use your computer to place a voice call to any telephone number worldwide, including mobiles. The cost of international voice calls on Skype is far lower than if you dial directly using your landline or mobile phone.

Does it cost anything to use Skype?

No, it is free to sign up and to install the software on your computer. You can also install a smartphone app that allows you to connect to Skype from your mobile. Calls between Skype users are free, and calls to non-Skype numbers worldwide are fairly low cost. You don't need to pay any subscription fees if you don't want to – a 'pay as you go' option allows you to add credit in small amounts, which you use each time you place a voice call. If you make frequent calls, it might be worth subscribing to the premium version, which offers unlimited calls to a country of your choice and a group video-call facility.

How do I join?

Go to skype.com and click on Join. Fill in the registration form and choose a Skype name (you can't change this later on so make sure you are happy with the name you choose) and a password. Alternatively, you can opt for the shortcut option of signing in via a Facebook or Microsoft account if you have one. You will then be able to download the software direct from the website and install it in the usual way.

Within a matter of seconds, you could be having the next best thing to a face-to-face chat with relatives thousands of kilometres away.

How do I make a call?

You open up Skype, and log in. You then add your contacts by clicking on **Add Contacts** and typing in each name or email address to see if the person is signed up to Skype – you can narrow your search to particular countries, cities, ages and so on. If you find someone you know, you send an invitation to add you to their contact list. Once they accept the invitation, you can call each other.

That seems really time-consuming. Is there a quicker way?

Click on the Contacts menu at the top of your screen. Select the option to **Import Contacts** and it will allow you to check the email addresses in your email program's address book if it is compatible. (You can't import email addresses on a Mac.)

My friend has accepted my invitation. How do I make a call?

Click on Contacts at the top left of the window. If your contact is online, there will be a green tick to the left of their name. Simply click on the green video-camera icon towards the right of their name to make a video call, or the green phone icon to make a voice-only call. If you make a voice-only call and want to turn it into a video call, then you can click on the video-camera icon once you are connected.

What happens if they don't want to talk to me? I wouldn't want to call them if they are busy (or in their pyjamas).

Theoretically, if your contact has a green tick next to their name, they are available – each person can change this tick to a 'Do not disturb' or 'Away' sign by clicking on the green tick icon at the top left of the window (you can choose to 'hide' as well, so that nobody can see you are online). But if you want to check this is a good time to call, send a message first: click on the blue message icon (like a speech bubble), and type your message into the long box that appears at the bottom of the window. Your contact will see the message and can then message you back, or call you.

Other ways to make contact

Skype has become a household name, but it is not the only option for making calls or sending messages over the internet.

Facetime, Apple's video-calling and video-messaging service, was first introduced for the iPhone in 2010. Users can make free face-to-face calls over WiFi between a range of compatible Apple devices, including iPads, Macs and iPhones.

Viber is a smartphone app, available on iOS, Android, BlackBerry or Windows phones. You can message or make free voice and video calls to any of the 200 million Viber users worldwide. The app identifies users by phone number, so it lists everyone in your phone contacts list who is using the service.

WhatsApp Messenger is a smartphone app, available on iOS, Android, BlackBerry or Windows phones. It allows you to text or send videos, audio files or images to other users over the internet. Like Viber, it will list anyone in your contacts list who is signed up. There's a small annual fee after a trial period.

Instant messaging (commonly known as IM or Chat) allows you to send messages online – it's basically texting on the internet. Messages are received, read and (probably) replied to instantly if your contacts are online. Yahoo! Messenger and AOL Messenger are two popular services; you also get a similar facility on social-media sites such as Facebook and Google+ (see Chapter 4).

4

SOCIAL NETWORKING

Starting points

- **Social networking** allows you to link up online with people you know in the real world – and people you don't.
- **It's incredibly popular**: in 2012, almost 70 per cent of US internet users belonged to a social network.
- **Facebook** has the most members. It began as a network for Harvard college students and now has more than a billion users worldwide.
- **There are social networks** specifically for work colleagues, photo enthusiasts, craft enthusiasts.
- **When you join a social network,** you have a dedicated page called a profile, which has your name, photograph and other information about yourself.

KEY ACTIONS

- Get started on Facebook.
- Find out about Google+, LinkedIn and other social networks.
- Take our mini master-class on Twitter.
- Customise your security settings to protect your information.
- Learn the dos and don'ts of networking online.

SOCIAL NETWORKING BASICS

What is the point of social networking?

It's fun! It's an easy way to keep up with people that you know – especially if you don't see each other or live in different areas of the country or world. You can find out in an instant that, say, your cousin has a new job, or you can view the photographs of a friend's wedding. And you can reconnect with people you have lost touch with – old school friends, relatives, former neighbours and so on.

I can do all that by email, can't I?

Yes, of course. But if email is like a private correspondence, then social networking is more of a conversation taking place in a room filled with your invited friends. Everything that the members of the group have to say can be shared with everyone else – because they 'post' their news on a page that all their connections have access to. That can be lively and stimulating and it will tend to be light-hearted.

But a social network is not just an online party or gossip circle. There are networks, and groups within networks, that focus on more narrow or more serious matters: specific hobbies such as reading or photography; political activism and campaigning; charity work; making professional or career-based connections. Any activity that is enjoyed as an online group, or that might bring people together as a group, can benefit from a social network. Obviously there will still be things that you want to say to one person in private. That too can be done on a social network (it's called private messaging, or PM for short) – but this is perhaps where email is preferable, because there is less chance of your correspondence leaking out by accident.

Isn't social networking for teenagers?

It was young people who first cottoned on to social networking, and yes, it is still the case that many users are in their 20s and younger. But that doesn't mean that social networking has nothing to offer you. These days the sites are used by people of all ages and from all walks of life. To give an example, the number of people over 65 who use social networking sites tripled from 2009 to 2013 in the USA – 43 per cent have now joined up.

Sites for sharing with friends

Here are some of the most popular social networking sites on the web. They all require you to register your details, and allow you to share your thoughts, images, videos or news. If you use a phone or tablet, they are best accessed via a dedicated app that you download.

Facebook

The biggest social networking site, Facebook helps you to find people you know and add them as 'friends'. Users have their own page, where they can write short updates ('posts') about what they are doing, or put links to, say, websites, videos or news stories for friends to view. You can also send messages in an instant to one or more of your contacts via the site. Many other sites let you sign in via your Facebook account rather than creating a separate account each time.

Twitter

Twitter users post short messages called tweets, which cannot be more than 140 characters long. Many people find something very appealing about having to express their thoughts in this succinct and strictly limited way. Because they are brief and instantaneous, tweets often take the form of pithy musings on current events. You can tweet your own thoughts and news, and you can 'follow' people whose tweets you like: friends, family, celebrities, journalists or politicians. The fact that public figures tweet means that Twitter is sometimes the place to keep up with what is happening as headline stories unroll.

Google+

Like most networking sites, Google+ allows you to add connections, share photographs and links, post messages and so on. On Google+ you organise your connections in Circles – you may have one each for friends, family, acquaintances, and others for, say, your work, or particular areas of interest: cooking, gardening, books. This means you can look at, say, your Gardening circle to see lots of updates from fellow enthusiasts, and then switch to your Friends circle to catch up on the latest from people you know in real life.

Instagram and Snapchat

These are popular apps for mobile devices. Instagram, owned by Facebook, allows you to upload photos or videos and edit them by adding a filter or frame. You 'follow' people you know or people whose work you admire, so that their images appear in your news feed, and you can 'like' them or add comments. Most images and videos can be viewed by anyone browsing the site, but you can also send them to one or more individuals via a message. This feature is similar to the one offered by the app Snapchat, in which you send images or videos to other users; these can be viewed only for a short, set period – preventing the recipients from saving it or passing it on to others.

Pinterest

Pinterest is like an online pinboard – you collect online images and put them together on a virtual board for others to see, comment on, or repin on their own boards. You follow other users' boards for inspiration – these can be people you know in real life, or just people with whom you share an interest. People use Pinterest for creating wishlists and for wedding and other event planning.

Myspace

Myspace was once the most visited social networking site in the world, but it has been overtaken by Facebook and others. It has always had a strong music emphasis (it is now partly owned by singer Justin Timberlake) and its main focus is to connect artists and fans.

Tumblr

Like Twitter, Tumblr users share their thoughts with followers. Tumblr allows longer posts and also displays images and audio and video content easily. Once signed up, you can follow people you know or those who talk about subjects that interest you – architecture, film, food and so on. Recent posts from people you follow are displayed on your 'Dashboard', and you can comment, like or share the post on this or another site. Posts tend to be quite short, fun, slightly anarchic.

LinkedIn

LinkedIn is networking for businesspeople. On your profile, you create an online CV in which you list your jobs, achievements, and current and former workplaces. LinkedIn suggests members who have also listed those places, and so might be present or former colleagues – allowing you to keep track of work contacts as they change jobs. LinkedIn has many professional groups that you can join. You can also link your profile to your website and add news updates.

How do I know which site is the right one for me?

If you feel unclear about whether you are going to like social networking it's probably a good idea to try Facebook first. It is the most popular site globally, and you are bound to know other people who use it. But new, and often niche, sites are being launched all the time. Some take off, some don't – and it's not easy to predict which sites will be successful. Ask your friends which ones they use or try searching the site with the names of a few people who are likely users. If nobody you know is there, it probably won't be much use... at least, not yet.

Do I have to pay for it?

Social networking sites are free, and that is one of their attractions. They make most of their money from the advertising that appears on the site. That advertising is automatically 'targeted' at individual users: when you use Facebook, for example, you will see advertisements that reflect the interests you reveal on your page.

FACEBOOK – IS IT FOR ME?

My friends keep sending me emails asking me to join Facebook, but I am not sure what it is or whether I want to be involved.

Before you can say whether Facebook is for you, you have to understand how it works. So here goes: first of all, Facebook is the biggest social network on the internet – it has around 1.2 billion members. It's a site where you can track down old acquaintances, share news and photographs with friends and family, organise social events... basically it is a way to communicate with lots of people that you know in cyberspace, all at once. And it's a two-way thing: everyone in your network can respond to your news instantly, and you can reply just as fast.

I'm still not sure I like the idea of it.

It's not for everyone, true. Whether or not you will enjoy Facebook depends on two things:

- Are people you know already on Facebook? If you have friends and family who are using the site – and the chances are that you do – then it's an easy and fun way to keep in touch with their daily lives, however far away they live and no matter how rarely you see them.

- Will you be happy to share aspects of your life with lots of people you know, and to be on the receiving end of other people's day-to-day news? Facebook needn't take up much of your time, but you'll get more out of it if you dip in regularly. So ask yourself if you care to update your 'profile' with news of what you are doing, or your thoughts on life – and if you are interested in reading what other people are up to.

If that sounds appealing,then give it a try. You can always close down your account on Facebook or any social networking site if you later find that it is not your thing.

Everyone in your network can respond to your news instantly, and you can reply just as fast.

Signing up to Facebook

How do I join Facebook?

To use the site, you need an account. Go to facebook.com, and fill out your basic details – your name, email address, date of birth and a password. This will start the registration process. At the end of the process, an email will be sent to you explaining how to activate the account. If you are on a phone or tablet, first download the Facebook app.

Facebook is asking to search my email account. Should I give permission?

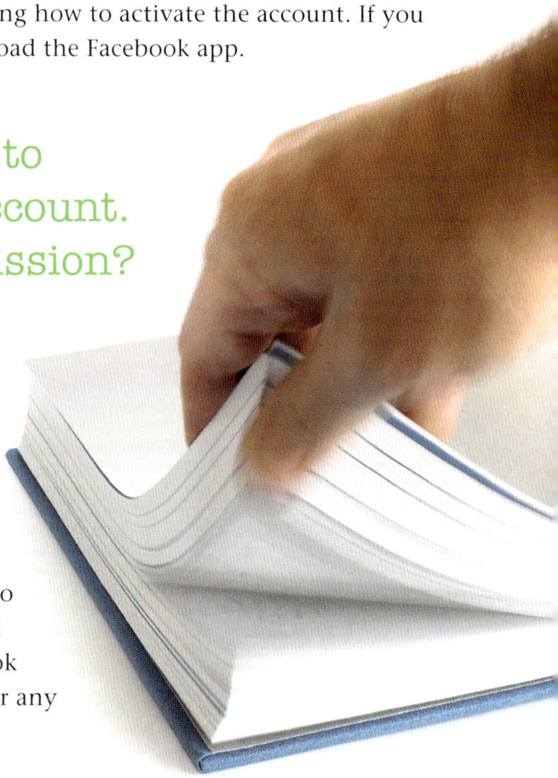

That depends. The point of Facebook is to connect with people you know. And the quickest way to find those people is to give the website permission to import your contacts' email addresses – which is what it is asking to do. But you can do this at any stage, and there are other ways to find people on the site. So if you feel uncomfortable about letting Facebook have access to your email account for any reason, just skip this stage.

I'll say yes, just for the fun of seeing who else is on Facebook.

Okay. You'll now see a list of people you know – each with his or her name and usually a picture too. Click on the **Add friend** button next to anyone you want to contact. It's a good idea to decide now whether you want to keep your Facebook account for friends and family, or whether you want to include work colleagues and clients. If in doubt, stick to people you know very well – you can always widen your circle of contacts later on.

The more information you add, the easier it will be for you to find people you know on Facebook and for them to find you.

Should I fill in all the background information it wants?

Facebook asks for basic information about you – where you grew up, where you live, where you work and so on – but it is entirely up to you how much you share. You might be happy to include your home town, for example, but not your school or workplace. If you are not sure, you can skip this stage altogether (again, you can add the information later). But the more information you add, the easier it will be for you to find people you know on Facebook and for them to find you.

Do I have to add a photo?

It is definitely worth adding a photograph of yourself to help people find you on Facebook. Unless you have an incredibly unusual name, there will be others on the site who share it – and a photograph will allow your friends to distinguish you from someone else. You can upload a favourite snap, or take one now with your computer's webcam. But, of course, you don't have to add a photo – you can use a picture of, say, your garden or a cartoon character or you can leave the space blank for now.

Customising your profile

I have my account. What do I do next?

Before you do anything, tighten up your security. The default settings on Facebook make your page – and everything you put on it – accessible to everyone. So you need to change your privacy settings – click on the little padlock icon at the top right of your page. There are two aspects to this:

1. Who can see your page? The default settings allow anyone to see everything on your page (called a 'profile'). The safest option is to make your information available to **Friends** only. **Friends of friends** may seem like a good option, because theoretically they are people your friends know. But bear in mind that many people are unselective about who they have as friends on Facebook – do you want your young nephew's school friends or your neighbour's ex-boyfriend viewing everything you post, for example?

2. Who can get in contact with you? Unless you have a particular reason to restrict this, it makes sense to allow **Everyone** to send you friend requests and to have **Basic Filtering** on your messages. That way, it is easy for people who know you to get in touch. Facebook filters the messages, so you shouldn't get spam in your inbox.

That was simple. Is that really it?

That's the shortcut. If you click on the gear icon next to the padlock one, there is a more complicated set of options where you have the choice of restricting still further what people can see. Once you have learned more about using Facebook, go into the privacy settings here and check that you are happy with them.

STAY SECURE

One crucial thing to remember is that Facebook can – and does – change its privacy policy from time to time. Make a point of checking your settings every so often, and certainly whenever Facebook notifies you of a change in its procedures.

What additional information should I add about myself?

The information you provided when you signed up is already on your profile, and you can now add more information on where you were born and went to school, where you live and work and your likes and dislikes. You can add as much information as you feel comfortable with – some people keep their Facebook data to the absolute minimum; others enjoy sharing a lot of information: the books they like, the music they listen to, and TV shows they watch, for example. To edit your information:

- Click on your name at the top right of the screen to get into your profile.
- Click on the **About** tab. You should see all the information you have entered at the signing-in stage, with the **Edit** button next to each entry.
- Click on **Edit** and fill in as much information as you like for each section. If you don't want to display the information on your profile, leave it blank.
- A pop-up window may appear, asking for more details. For example, if you add your place of work, you can now fill in the position you hold, where your work is located and so on.
- When you are done, click on the blue button at the bottom of the window, then click on **Done editing** and move on to the next section.

Finding friends

How do I find people I know?

The site makes it easy to find friends by generating suggestions based on the information you have provided and the friends you have already. Don't be surprised to see photographs of work colleagues, ex-partners or forgotten schoolmates pop up on your screen.

- When you first join, you are automatically directed to the welcome page, which contains a list of friend suggestions. All you need to do is to click on the **Add Friend** button to send an invitation.

- If you are on your home page or profile page, click on the **Find Friends** button at the top right of the screen. Here you will find a list of **People you may know** plus a list of anyone who has sent you a friend request that you haven't responded to yet. You can fill in your email address if you want Facebook to search your email contacts for users of the site. It also allows you to search for people who have added a specific workplace, home town or similar to their information. And it gives you the option to invite a specific friend or acquaintance to join Facebook by filling in his or her email address or name.

- To check if a particular person is on Facebook, type his or her name into the blank search bar at the top of your screen. A list of people with that name will pop up on your screen. Find the right person by looking at the photograph shown (or at the list of friends associated with that account), then click on the **Add Friend** button to make contact.

Someone who has hundreds of friends is much less likely to notice your absence than someone with just a handful.

Can I get rid of a friend once I have added him or her?

Yes, you can. It's easy to 'unfriend' someone. Simply go to their profile page and click on the gear icon at the far right of his or her name, then click **Unfriend**.

Will the person know I have done that? I don't want to hurt anyone's feelings.

No notification is sent out when you unfriend someone, so he or she won't automatically realise that you have removed yourself. But your name will no longer appear in his or her friends' list, and this might be noticed eventually; someone who has hundreds of friends is much less likely to notice your absence than someone with just a handful.

I don't want to unfriend my neighbour, but she posts dull updates every hour. Is there a way of removing them?

You can hide someone's updates very easily. Simply let your cursor hover over his or her post; an arrow will appear in the top-right corner. Click on this, and you have the option to hide a particular post or all posts from this person. If you want to report a post as spam or containing offensive or upsetting content, follow the same procedure and then select the option you want.

I hid someone and now I quite miss the updates! Can I get them back?

It's quite common to regret hiding someone's posts. To get your friend's posts back, go to your home page and let your cursor hover over **News Feed** in the left-hand menu. When the little pencil (the edit icon) appears, click on it and then click on **Edit Settings**. A list of friends and apps that you have hidden appears; to reinstate their posts, click on the **X** next to their name and press the **Save** button. Their status updates should again appear in your news feed from now on.

Courteous networking

Like all online communities, social networks have their own etiquette. Here are six key rules to bear in mind.

1. Remember who you are speaking to. There may be things you would say to one Facebook friend, and perhaps language that you would use, which you wouldn't dream of letting other friends overhear. Bear in mind that, generally, all your friends are in on the conversation, and that may include people who should only really see your 'serious' face.

2. Don't worry about refusing invitations. It's perfectly acceptable to turn down a request (perhaps with a polite 'sorry, I keep this account for family only', for example) or to ignore it altogether. Likewise, don't be offended if your invitation goes unanswered.

3. Separate home and work. It can be a good idea to connect with work acquaintances only on work-related sites such as LinkedIn. If you do have colleagues on social networks, then consider using the settings to make sure that they don't get all the pictures of your riotous birthday party.

4. Be photo-selective. Don't tag people in photographs that show them in an unbecoming light – it could cause them difficulty at work or home. It's best to be very selective about the photographs you post online in any case.

5. Think before you post. Don't write anything critical, personal or insulting about someone you know (or don't know, come to that). Comments can travel very easily. Be especially careful when saying anything about your work, colleagues (or boss) or clients. Avoid gossiping, and don't post anything that might offend or upset people in your network, or in friends' networks. It is all too easy to embarrass yourself or, more seriously, to say something that could expose you to charges of libel.

6. Don't update too often. Few things are duller than a Facebook friend who tells you what they are having for breakfast. Be selective about what you post, and make it interesting.

Updating your profile

I'm ready to get started. How do I let people know what I am doing?

When you log into Facebook, go to **News Feed**, which is basically a list of all the latest updates, photographs and links that your friends have posted. To post your own update, type a sentence or two into the **What's on your mind?** box (under **Update Status**) and then click on the **Post** button.

I am on a different page. How do I get to my news feed?

There is a menu of options on the left of your screen – click on **News Feed**. Alternatively, click on **Home** at the top right of the blue menu bar that runs across your screen. You can also update your status from your profile page – click on your name on the same blue menu bar.

I don't know what to say! Any suggestions for my first post?

People say anything and everything on Facebook, as you will soon discover. Scroll through your news feed, and see what your friends are talking about to give you some ideas. You can share family news, talk about the latest film you have seen or say what you doing right now – but try to make it interesting and personal: 'Just been picking the roses: white ones always reminds me of my mother, who loved them so much.' 'Has anyone else read *The Master and Margarita*? I'd never heard of it, but it's a wonderful novel.', 'Just finished making a birthday cake for my granddaughter's 6th birthday.' Or maybe you want to write a quick message about being new to Facebook – 'Have finally arrived on Facebook!' usually elicits some welcoming responses.

Scroll through your news feed and see what your friends are saying, to give you ideas about what to post.

Shhhh!
What not to share

It's fun to use social networks, but a detailed online persona can make you vulnerable to unscrupulous people. Even if you have strict privacy settings in place, it is still possible that your account or that of a contact could be broken into, giving others access to personal information.

It is also possible for things that you have deleted to live on: friends may have passed on snippets or saved your posts by making screenshots (photographs of the display on their screen), for example. So be careful about what you share in the first place. Here are four things you might want to keep to yourself:

- **Your date of birth.** It's lovely to get birthday wishes from friends online, true. But this is one of the key pieces of information needed for identity theft. Your date of birth is automatically added to your profile when you sign up – so it is accessible to everyone who can see your page. To remove it, go to your profile page, click on **Update Info**, and then click **Edit** next to your birthday and change the settings so that only you can see this information. At the very least, hide the year of birth.

- **Where you are.** Lots of people use a facility known as 'signing in' on the site, revealing exactly where they are. But letting everyone know that you are not at home is never a good idea. Keep your location private. Likewise, don't broadcast the fact you are home alone.

- **Your holiday plans.** Don't post updates such as 'Off to Bali for a fortnight – so excited!', and don't use Facebook to request house-sitters! Why give burglars any kind of useful lead?

- **Pictures of children with their full names.** Many Facebook users post pictures of children. But posting an up-to-date photograph along with the name of a child and access to the names of friends and family is not sensible. If you post photographs of children, be sure to restrict the audience and don't tag the pictures. Don't post images of other people's children unless you know they are happy for you to do so.

Then what?

Friends may click the 'Like' button – which looks like a thumbs-up – underneath your status update to show that they have seen it and enjoyed reading it, or they may leave a comment underneath. You can add your own comment, and a whole conversation may ensue. But don't worry if nobody says anything – some posts spark lots of interest, others just float away, like a message in a bottle.

I said something dumb, and now I feel embarrassed. Can I delete it?

Everyone gets the occasional flash of Facebook regret. If you want to delete your update, you can. Simply let your mouse hover over the top right-hand side of the post, and a little blue cross appears. Click on this and your post disappears. You can delete any comments you make on other people's profiles in exactly the same way – though, of course, they may already have read your comment by the time you do that.

Some of your posts may spark lots of interest, others just float away, like a message in a bottle.

I have lots of work colleagues as friends. Is there a way of restricting what they see on my Facebook page?

Facebook has a useful Lists feature, which means you can organise your friends into work colleagues, family and so on. Some friends are added automatically to a list depending on their profile information – for example, if you have listed a particular workplace, any friends who have done the same will be added to a list for that place. You have to add friends manually to other lists. To do this:

- Go to your profile page. Click on the **Friends** tab at the top of the page.

- Next to each friend's name will be a ticked box, with the default option of **Friends**. Click on this box and select, say, **Acquaintances**.

- To add to a different list, click on **Add to another list** and either select one of the lists generated by Facebook or **+New List** to create a new customised one.

Now when you add a status update that you want to restrict to a certain group, click on the **Friends** button next to **Post**. A drop-down menu appears: select the group of friends who should see your update (**Friends except Acquaintances** is one useful option), then press **Post** as usual. In this example, anyone designated an acquaintance will not see your update.

Adding links and photographs

I've just read a brilliant news article online, and want to let my friends know about it. Is that easy to do?

It is. Simply go to the address bar and press **Ctrl/Cmd+C** to copy the web address. Then paste the website address into your status box, by pressing **Ctrl/Cmd+V**, and add a comment if you want to. The page you are linking to appears in a box below your status. You can also add a link to a favourite web-based video clip – such as something from YouTube.

How about adding a photo?

Sharing photographs often elicits more response than a written status update by itself. Click on **Add Photos/Video** next to **Status Update**, and a window allowing you to browse the files on your computer will appear. Find the photograph you want, then click on the **Choose** or **Open** button. The picture should appear in your status box. Add a comment about the picture and then press the **Post** button. You can add a short video in the same way.

I want to upload a whole set of photographs from my friend's wedding. It will take ages to upload them one by one. Is there a quicker way?

Yes, you can upload multiple photographs, and create an album to put them into. Put all the images in the same folder on your hard drive first.

- Click on **Add Photo/Video** and choose the **Create Photo Album** option.
- Find the photographs you want. To select more than one image file, hold down the **shift** key as you click. Then click **Choose** or **Open**.
- A window pops up, allowing you to give the album a title and to add a comment as well as details of where and when the photographs were taken.
- At the bottom of your screen you will see a progress bar showing how long your album will take to upload. Once the upload is complete, you can choose to upload more photographs and change the settings for who is able to see the photographs. Click the blue **Post Photos** button.

I'm being asked to 'tag' a photograph. What is tagging?

Tagging is adding a label to a photograph to identify who is in it. If you tag someone in a photograph, the image will automatically appear on his or her news feed as well as your own – this means, of course, that his or her own friends can see it and like or comment on it. Your friend also has the option of deleting it from his or her feed or removing the tag.

Can I tag a photograph as I upload it?

When you upload a photograph, you automatically get the option to 'tag' friends who appear in the photograph. Start to type the name into the box below each photograph and a list of your friends' names will appear. You can tag a photograph with names of your friends (or any public figures with a Facebook page). Click on the one you want, then click on **Save Tags**. If you don't want to tag, click on **Skip tagging friends**.

Can I tag a photograph that I have already uploaded?

Yes. Just click on the photograph, then **Tag Photo**. Click on the person you want to tag. Start typing their name into the box that appears and then click on his or her name as it appears in the list below. Click **Done Tagging**. If you want to change or delete the tag, click the photograph, then click on **Edit**.

Can I delete a photo I have uploaded?

To delete a photo that you have uploaded, go to your photos page (you'll find a clickable link to this in the left-hand menu when you are on the home page). Let your mouse hover over the photo and then click on the pencil icon that appears in the right-hand corner: this gives you the option to edit or delete it. You can also click on **Albums**, and then **Edit** to delete the album, edit the photographs or change the album name and details.

If you tag someone in a photograph, the image will automatically appear on his or her news feed as well as your own.

What's it all about... Google+

Google+ (plus.google.com) is the name of Google's social networking site. Like Facebook, it allows you to create your own profile page, find contacts, post updates, send messages, share links and so on. You can also easily follow news organisations, celebrities or special-interest groups. You use the same log-in details for Google+ that you do for other Google services (Gmail, YouTube and so on). Here are the key features:

- **Circles** You group your contacts, or any other Google+ members that you are interested in, into Circles: you might have a Friends circle, Acquaintances circle, Work circle, Hobby circle, for example. (Your contacts do not know how you have grouped them, and you can put people into more than one group.) Your circles are listed in a menu at the top of your screen, so you can flick between them with one click. This makes it very easy to post an update to a particular group, or to take a look at what has been posted by people or companies that you have placed in that group. You only see posts by people if they have shared them publicly, or if they have added you to a particular circle.

- **Communities** Like LinkedIn and Facebook, Google+ has groups that share a particular interest or activity – Italian cooking, self-publishing, Dr Who, and many, many more. These are called Communities and you can join as many as you wish. You can browse the news page (called the 'stream') of a community, and once you are a member you can add comments. The design of Google+ is clever and pleasing – so reading news pages feels rather like reading a mini online magazine that is constantly updated. Google+ also has a 'What's Hot' section that shows popular posts on the site.

- **Hangouts** You can use Hangouts to have an online conversation with a group of people (like a conference call). Each participant appears on your screen – when a person is talking, his or her picture gets larger, only to become smaller again when the next person starts talking, as if he or she were stepping centre-stage to say their piece. As well as having a group video chat, you can share video links. Hangouts is a good facility to use if you are working up an idea – planning a wedding, say, or getting a set list together for your band's reunion gig – and want to share it with several people in different places. You can access Hangouts from a computer and also via the Google+ app on a phone or tablet – so you can start a conversation from your computer and then continue it on your phone if you need to go out. Mobile users can also use the service for group text messaging.

- **Instant upload of photographs from your phone.** You can upload as many photographs as you like to Google+. You can set your phone to automatically upload photographs to the site if you have a Google+ app, and allow **Instant Upload.** When you upload photographs to Google+, they first go into a private folder – which is in effect an online storage facility. You can then organise them into different albums and decide who to share them with.

Catching up with friends

How do I read my friends' updates?

Your friends' status updates will appear in your news feed, unless you choose to hide them. Their names will appear in blue on your feed. You can also visit any friend's profile page: click on his or her name to be directed there. Alternatively, start to type their name into the search bar at the top of your screen, then click on that particular friend from the list that is generated. You can post a comment on your friend's profile, or simply look at the comments, images and links that are there.

I want to write something to my friend but I don't want anyone else to see it. Is there a way of doing that?

Yes, there are several ways of sending a private message on Facebook. Try this:

- Go to your home page. Click on **Messages** in the left-hand menu.
- Click on **+New Message** at the top right of the window.
- Start to type the name of the recipient in the To: box, and then click on the name of that person from the list that is generated.
- Type your message in the message box at the bottom of the window – you can attach a link or photograph here if you like – then press the blue **Reply**.

What's the difference between doing that and sending an email?

One good thing about sending messages on Facebook is that your messages and your friend's replies are displayed in a rolling conversation. So you can scroll back to see messages from months or even years back. And you can message two or more friends at once, and everyone can see everyone else's replies. It is a useful way to, say, arrange a night out with a group of people. And, of course, you don't need to type in an email address.

What are the other ways of sending a message?

There's a Chat facility at the bottom right of your window. Click on this and a sidebar appears showing which of your friends are online at any given moment. If there's a green circle by the name, he or she is online; a phone icon means that he or she uses the Facebook app on a mobile device; and if there is no icon, he or she is not on Chat (and messages will be sent directly to his or her inbox). Click on the friend you want to contact (or use the search bar to find a friend who is not listed) and a small message box appears – you can then send a quick message and wait for a (hopefully instant) response. It is surprising how much fun it is to have an online conversation like this – it's a version of the old thrill you got from passing notes to and fro at the back of the classroom. As with messaging, you can talk to more than one friend at once.

I'm not sure I want everyone to know when I am on Facebook, though.

It is easy to switch off Chat. All you need to do is:

- Click on the gear icon in the Chat sidebar (it's at the bottom right of your screen).
- Click on **Turn Off Chat**.

Alternatively, click on **Advanced Settings**, which allows you to stop some friends from knowing when you are online and restrict Chat to a chosen few. You can still message anyone using Chat if you do this.

I've seen pages that are not about individuals, but about businesses and public bodies. What's the point of them?

All sorts of organisations have a Facebook page that they use for advertising or publicising their activity. There will be one for your library or arts group, your council, charities and action groups, local businesses such as plumbers, electricians or window cleaners. This is not what Facebook was invented for, but such pages are a resource that you might as well use. If you like a page, you will receive its status updates – so it can be a good way of finding out about events in your area or supporting a political or charitable cause you believe in. And if you have a business, or an upcoming event, you can set up a Facebook page to promote it.

I want to have a school reunion. I guess Facebook is a handy tool for that.

Facebook has made event planning so much easier – you can set up a single page with all the details and invite all your friends to come. And, depending on how you set up the page, your friends can then send invitations to their connections, and so on. To create an Event page:

- From the home page, select **Events** from the left-hand menu.
- Click on +**Create Event** at the top right.
- Add the event name and a comment about it. Then start typing the location – a list of options will come up; choose the right one (you can manually input the location if necessary, too). Add the date and time, then choose who the event is open to: invited guests only (**Invite Only**), invitees and their friends (**Friends of Guests**) or everyone (**Public Event**).
- If you choose to make the event Invite Only, you can allow your guests to invite their friends by ticking the box below (**Guests can invite friends**).
- Click on the blue **Invite Friends** link in the bottom left-hand corner.
- Your event page will appear. You can now choose to add a photograph (**Add Event Photo**), **Invite Friends** or edit any of the event details.
- Guests you invite have the option of replying **Yes**, **No** or **Maybe**, so you know who is planning to come.

Neater networking

If you spend a lot of time flicking from one social-media site to another when you are on a phone or tablet, then you may want to combine them in a single app.

You can use what's called a social media aggregator. One such is Flipboard – an app that works with Apple, Android and other devices.

How does it work?

Once you have downloaded the app, you can create a Flipboard account or simply sign in through your Facebook or Twitter account. Then you select any social networking sites you belong to from the menu, type in the relevant user name and password, and allow Flipboard to access each account. You can then flick between feeds of different accounts, both to view and to post updates.

Why would I use it?

It is designed to be easy and pleasing to read so it feels more like reading an online magazine than scrolling through a news feed. And it not only allows you to access your social networking sites, but gives you access to articles from magazines and news sources – Harper's Bazaar, W magazine, BBC News, to give a few examples. You can 'bookmark' articles that you like, and organise them into 'Magazines' to read later or to share with others. It's an enjoyable way to view the things you are interested in – both from your personal life and the wider world – in one neat package.

A GUIDE TO TWITTER

A lot of my friends are on Twitter, but I don't get it. What's it all about?

Twitter is a forum in which people send short pithy messages, which are strictly limited to no more than 140 characters. And since the messages are so short and they can be read the instant they are sent, Twitter tends to be totally up-to-the-minute, which gives it an immediacy and excitement. Here are four ways you might want to use Twitter:

It's a good way of following news in realtime. Say an election is going on – you can find out what is happening and also read comments by all sorts of different Twitter users minute-by-minute – just as the events unfold. So you are not just learning what a particular journalist or political pundit thinks (as on the TV), you can also get the perspective of your best friend, your aunt, favourite comedian, top celebrities and so on – all distilled into one short sentence each. You might answer, disagree, resend their message to your own friends to see what their response is... Being on Twitter has been likened to being at a cocktail party full of people who interest you – where the conversation is fast-moving and often witty.

You can keep tabs on people you know (and people you don't). You can use it to keep up with the daily musings of people you know and love, and also with people you are interested in – celebrities, sportspeople, scientists. The fun is getting the news from the horse's mouth, and straight away: just as you are setting out for the school run, you get a message from Stephen Fry saying that he is on location in Greece, making a new film...

You can find out about developments or events that you are interested in. Say you like tennis or chess or knitting or science. There will be people who send messages about these topics, and many of the organisations and companies involved in these areas send messages, too. And you can find out specifically about things in your local area – your local government, charities, arts and sports organisations, libraries and so on are all likely to tweet about what they are doing.

And sometimes Twitter is just good for a laugh – a favourite comedian might post a funny joke, or a friend might tweet everyone to say that she just remembered it was her husband's birthday yesterday...

Getting started on Twitter

How do I sign up, and do I have to pay?

Getting a Twitter account is easy, and it is free. Users access Twitter through the website interface, SMS, or mobile device app. If you are on a mobile device, download the app; otherwise go to twitter.com. Sign up by entering your name, email address and a password in the **New to Twitter?** box. Then click the **Sign up for Twitter** button.

- You'll then be asked to choose a username, and to click on a **Create My Account** button.

- You will then need to copy some digits into a box and agree to the Twitter terms and conditions before clicking on the **Create My Account** button again.

- Check your email address for Twitter's confirmation email – take a look in your junk mail folder if it is not in your inbox – and click on the link to confirm the account.

What username shall I choose?

If your real name is available, you can use it, of course – this will help friends and acquaintances find you on Twitter. Otherwise you can have anything you like as your Twitter name – a version of your own name (Clarkie or JClarkson, for Jane Clarkson, say) to something completely made up (Gardengnome, Ilovereading).

Can I change my name later on?

Yes, you can change your name as often as you like. To change it:

- Simply log on, click on the gear icon in the top-right corner, and choose **Settings** from the drop-down menu.

- Fill in your new username in the box.

- Click on the **Save Changes** button at the bottom of the page.

Remember to let your followers know you have changed your name – the easiest way is to tweet them!

At-a-glance guide to Twitter-speak

There's no denying that Twitter seems confusing when you are new to it. That's because users have a set of abbreviations to help them convey their messages as briefly as possible, in the required 140 characters. Here are the shortcuts you need to know about.

 # Hashtags are key to tweeting. It's a way of flagging the subject under discussion. Once a word is labelled with a hashtag, other users can search for it and find all the posts containing that word or phrase. So you might write a tweet in which the hashtag is part of the sentence 'Looking forward to the #oscarstonight'; or it can be a separate label such as 'Wondering what plants thrive best in shady sites #gardening'. Many tweeters makes jokes of their hashtags: 'So it's raining at the Wimbledon final #notnews.'

@ The @ symbol followed by a user's name crops up a lot. It's a way of alerting a Twitter user to the fact they're mentioned in a tweet, and may encourage that user to respond; it's also used to name-check celebrities who are on Twitter. So you may see '@barackobama gave a great speech last night'.

RT This stands for retweet – meaning that a user has passed a tweet on to his or her own followers. Retweeting is part of the fun of Twitter. A successful tweet is one that is much retweeted. The format is: RT@username (that is, the username of the person who wrote the tweet in the first place) and then the tweet.

MT If a user has retweeted but has changed the original tweet slightly – usually so that he or she can add a comment to it but still keep within the 140 characters – you will see MT rather than RT. It stands for modified tweet.

HT Short for hat tip. This rather quaint abbreviation is a way of complimenting or crediting the user who originally shared a blog or link. The form is to put HT followed by @username.

OH This means overheard – it's common to tweet funny or strange comments that Twitter users have heard in real life. Sometimes RLRT – signifying real life retweet – is used.

TIL Meaning 'Today I learned', this can be a good way to start a tweet. 'TIL what a hashtag is', for example.

TT Any topic or # might become very popular on Twitter – this is dubbed a trending topic, or TT. You will find a list of personalised trending topics, based on your location and who you follow, on your Twitter page. You can opt to see TTs for a particular location if you prefer – press the blue **Change** link to do this.

Should I upload a photo of myself?

Most Twitter users upload an image. As with Facebook, it helps people to find you, and it adds personality to your profile. You don't have to choose a photograph of yourself if you don't want to; any image that you feel represents you or your interests will do.

I need to write a few words for the bio section. What should I say?

When you first join Twitter, you are asked to write a mini-biography (a bio). You have 160 characters to paint a word-picture of yourself. This can be your job, your characteristics, your roles in life, your interests. Think of it as answering these questions:

- Who am I?
- What do I do?
- What am I interested in?

So a bio might be something like: 'Stressed-out teacher, gardener, procrastinator' or 'Grandmother of six – and advertising executive', 'New Yorker living in Melbourne'. The bio is almost a kind of advertisement for yourself, and indicator of the tone and theme of the things you are going to tweet. Have some fun creating your bio, and bear in mind that (generally speaking) Twitter is a light-hearted and pithy medium. So don't make your bio read like a potted version of your CV.

Who should I connect with on Twitter?

Anyone who interests you. You certainly don't have to know people in real life to connect with them on Twitter. Basically you 'follow' anyone who intrigues you in some way – whether they are friends, family, work colleagues, celebrities, journalists, comedians, politicians, sportspeople. You can also follow companies, groups and organisations.

What happens when I follow someone?

Once you follow Twitter users, their messages (tweets) appear automatically on your feed. And if they follow you back, your tweets will appear on their feeds.

You can follow celebrities, sportspeople, journalists, companies, comedians, politicians...

How do I find people to follow?

There are a few ways of doing this:

1. Search on individual names or email addresses – type a name into the search bar at the top of the page, then select the right person from the list that appears below. (As you will see, the list is split into two – the top half consists of tweets where that person is mentioned; the bottom half are Twitter accounts relating to that name.) You can find celebrities, sportspeople, journalists, companies, comedians, politicians in this way – try searching for Paul McCartney, Barack Obama, Ian Thorpe, Pelé or Madonna, for example.

2. If there is a subject you are particularly interested in – tennis, gardening, knitting, architecture – type that into the search bar to find people who tweet about it. You'll find your favourite TV shows, newspaper, local events and local government in the same way – type in your home town, and see what comes up.

3. Import an address book from selected webmail accounts – which involves allowing Twitter access to that account:

- Click on **#Discover** from the menu at the top of the page.
- Click on **Find friends** from the menu on the left.
- Click on the **Search contacts** button next to your email account.
- Type in the user details to the account and click the blue **Sign in** button.

I'm importing my address book, but I don't want to follow all my contacts.

Be aware that when Twitter imports addresses from your email account, it automatically assumes you want to follow anyone who is already on Twitter. Unless you want to follow everyone in your address book, untick the **Select All** box at the top, then select individuals that you do want to follow by clicking on the tickbox next to their names.

You then get the option to invite any contacts not currently on Twitter to join. Again untick the **Select All** box and select individuals one by one. Or simply click on the **Skip this step** option.

Hardly anyone I know seems to be on Twitter, and I can't think of anyone to follow. Any suggestions?

Twitter generates suggestions for you based on who you already follow – click on the **Who to follow** option (again in **#Discover**) to find these. Click the **Follow** button for anyone that interests you.

I have followed someone by accident. How do I stop following a Twitter user?

You can 'unfollow' a Twitter user in an instant. Go to the user's profile page (to get there, start to type his or her name in the search bar at the top of the page, then select the right user from the list that is generated underneath). You will see a blue **Following** button at the top right of the page. Click on this, and it will turn to the grey **Follow** button (which means you are not currently following this user). If you want to re-follow at any point, click on the **Follow** button again.

If I really like a tweet, can I keep a record of it?

You can keep favourite Tweets: let your cursor hover over the tweet, then click on the star that appears. Go to your profile and click on **Favorites** in the left-hand menu to see them. The user can see who has favourited his or her tweet, so it is a way of complimenting him or her without sending a message (rather like Facebook's **Like** button).

How to tweet

I want to post a tweet...

Sign in to your Twitter account, and make sure you are on your home page (click on the little house icon at the top left of your screen to get there). Then click on the **Compose new Tweet** box on the left, or the blue compose icon at the top right of your screen. Type in the box that appears – you'll see the number of characters you have left at the bottom right – and click on the camera icon if you want to add an image stored on your device. When you have finished click on the blue **Tweet** button. Your tweets will appear in the news feed of anyone who follows you.

Who sees my tweets?

Your tweets get sent to anyone who follows you, and also to anyone you mention if you preface his or her username with the @ sign. But Twitter is a public forum so anyone can see your tweets if he or she searches for your username or for a word that appears in one of your tweets. If you don't want this to happen, then you can opt to **Protect my tweets** in your security settings – this means that you approve any request to follow you and only those people following you can access your tweets. If you want to check or change your security settings, go to the gear icon at the top right of the screen and select **Settings**. Then choose **Security and privacy** from the menu on the left. You can also prevent a specific user from seeing your tweets by going to his or her page and clicking on the head-and-shoulders icon next to the blue Follow button; select **Block @username**.

Twitter is a public forum so anyone can see your tweets if he or she searches for your username or for a word that appears in one of your tweets.

What on earth do I talk about?

Twitter doesn't have to be intimidating or complicated. It's just smalltalk for the digital age – but as in real life, a simple opening gambit can pave the way to a fruitful conversation. Here are some ideas to start with:

- Share good websites or articles that you spot on the web, or photographs or videos that you have taken or found online.

- Ask questions – 'What's the best advice your granny gave you?' – that may encourage your followers to reply.

- Repeat a joke that you have heard.

- Tweet about the news, events, or what is on the TV.

- Celebrate your achievements – whether you have baked a fabulous cake, met a deadline, finished a big project... Or if you have a cold or your car has been clamped or you have dropped a pile of plates, you can say so. You may get a bigger response than when you tweet about something good.

- Say what you are doing right now. A lot of tweets are simple sharings of the present moment – whether you are standing in the longest queue ever, having a beer in the sunshine, walking by the sea.

Is there anything I shouldn't say?

Tweeting is really a form of electronic publishing, so don't say anything that might have a legal implication. For example, if the media reports that there's been an injunction preventing them from naming, say, a celebrity who has had a secret love affair, and you know who that celebrity is, don't tweet it! People have been sued for doing precisely this. If you seem to encourage or admit to a crime ('Just broke the speed limit') you may get a visit from the police – in 2013 a UK driver who tweeted that she had hit a cyclist made national headlines when she was tweeted back by her local police station asking her to come and report the incident.

I want to add a link but it's so long it uses up my 140 characters on its own.

There are websites that shorten links for you. Go to bitly.com, to take one example, and set up an account. Once registered, you can paste links into a box on the site, and it will provide you with a truncated form, about ten characters long, that you can use in tweets – and also in emails and on websites. On the site you can also track how many people click on the short links that you have made – which is a good way of finding out how much interest you have generated. Other sites that provide a similar service are tinyurl.com and Google's goo.gl.

Can I tweet from my phone?

You can tweet using the Twitter app, which is free to download, if you have a smart phone. This is in fact how most people do it – on the move, in a spare moment, from a taxi, or during a coffee break... It is the fact that much tweeting happens in life's brief breathing spaces that gives this form of networking its edgy sense of urgency. Tweeting is all about what is happening *right now*.

How you use Twitter will depend on what you want to get out of it – and the key is to organise your feed.

I can't think of anything to say!

If you are not sure what to tweet about, you could start by replying to other people's tweets – agree, disagree, offer support, share a similar idea or experience. Or if you think someone has said something worth repeating, you can do exactly that – retweeting, as it is known on Twitter, is a great way to share something you've enjoyed with people who are following you.

How do I retweet something?

Retweeting is an integral part of Twitter. If you see a tweet that you want to pass on, move your cursor over it: this highlights both the tweet and the options below it. Click on the option **Retweet** and the tweet is automatically shared with your followers under the original author's name (the message 'Retweeted by yourusername' appears underneath). Alternatively, copy the tweet and paste it into your **Compose new Tweet** box. Type in any additional comments that you have, then the abbreviation RT followed by @username of the original author to acknowledge the source. If you need to shorten the tweet to stay within the 140-character limit, then use the abbreviation MT instead of RT. On some devices you get the option to **Quote tweet:** this does the pasting for you and lets you add a comment of your own.

How do I reply to someone?

Conversations spring up on Twitter all the time, and a surprising number of celebrities respond to their followers, too. If you want to reply to a tweet, you highlight the tweet as above, and then click on **Reply**. A box appears with @username of the original author and you type your reply after that. Your reply will be tweeted to anyone who follows you and the person you are replying to; it will also show up in the Mentions tab (which you will find if you click on @ **Connect** at the top of your screen. If you want to send a private reply, send a direct message instead.

I want to send a private message to someone I follow. Can I do that?

You can send private messages (direct messages) on Twitter, but only if you and the user both follow each other. Click on the envelope icon at the top right of your screen, and then click on **New message**. Start typing the username in the uppermost box and a list of your followers will appear. Select the right one, and then type your message in the box below (you're still restricted to 140 characters). Click the blue **Send message** button.

How can I delete a tweet I have posted?

Go to your profile page and your tweets will be on the right. Find the tweet and let your mouse hover over it. Various options including **Delete** will appear; click on this, then confirm you want to remove the tweet. If you want to delete a retweet, then let your mouse hover over it and select **Retweeted** – this will delete your tweet but not the original.

Getting more out of Twitter

I still find Twitter really confusing and a bit pointless – what am I missing?

When you first join Twitter, you tend to follow anyone and everyone who catches your eye. This can be fun – you never know whose messages are going to pop up on your feed – but it can also be dull, because you don't want to wade through dozens of tweets before you read something you are actually interested in. So the first thing to consider is why are you here? Do you want to keep up with friends and family? Follow your favourite celebrities? Follow journalists and comedians to get an irreverent take on news events as they happen? Be alerted to local events and offers?

How you use Twitter will depend on what you want to get out of it – and the real key is to organise your Twitter page so that it shows messages from people you like or find amusing or interesting. If that is not the case, consider unfollowing a few (or a lot of) users.

I follow my local public transport system. It's useful at times but I don't need to see every tweet. What can I do?

You can organise your Twitter people into lists, depending on who they are or what they tweet about – you may have a Friends list, a Family list, a News list, a Hobbies list and so on. To create a list:

- Click on the gear icon at the top right of the screen.
- From the drop-down menu that appears, choose **Lists**.
- Click on **Create list.**
- A new window appears: name your list, and add a short description of it (if you want to). Choose the privacy option **Private** (which means only you can access the list).
- Click **Save list**.

When you want to view tweets from a particular list, you go to your profile page and click on **Lists**, then select the list that you want to view. You will then see tweets from all the users in that list in your timeline.

How do I add new people to a list?

You add someone to the list by clicking on the head-and-shoulders icon next to the **Following** button on their profile; choose **Add or remove from list** and then in the new window that appears select the tickbox next to the list that you want to put them in; you can also create a new list at this point if you want to. Close the window by clicking on the X in the right-hand corner. (You can remove someone from a list by clicking on the tickbox again – this removes the tick.) You don't have to be following someone to add him or her to your list.

I see there is something called a public list. What's the point of that?

If your lists are just to help you organise your feed, there is no point at all. But you might like to make a list of, say, favourite comedians or romantic novelists. If you make it public, someone else may follow it – in which case it is added to their own lists. There is no real reason to do this – it's just one of the ways you can share your opinions with others.

ONLINE FORUMS

What is an online forum?

The web allows you to have a 'conversation' with people that you don't know but share an interest with through sites known as forums. You can find a forum for pretty much any subject – books, parenting, your particular brand of computer, the history of your local area, knitting, Labradoodle dogs (or any other breed), vintage motorcycles...

I've heard of chat rooms. Are they the same thing?

They are similar, but most chat rooms allow users to talk about anything and everything, while a forum focuses on a subject or interest. Forums also tend to be more strictly moderated, though this isn't always the case.

How are they moderated?

Sites usually have an administrator who ensures that inappropriate comments are removed. Any user can report a comment as inappropriate – it may be offensive or advertising, say – and the moderator may then delete it. Users who consistently make inappropriate comments may be blocked from the site (though there is nothing to stop them re-registering with a different email address, of course).

How do I find a forum that suits me?

The simplest way is to type the word 'forum' together with your chosen interest into your search engine. If you use Google, click on **More** underneath the search box, and select **Discussions**. This targets your search more precisely towards groups. Alternatively, try using the search engine omgili.com, which specifically focuses on forums, discussion groups and suchlike. There are many forums on the net, and some are a lot better than others, so check out a few before you find one you like. You can usually scroll through existing discussions to see what you think before you register as a user.

Know your netiquette

Different online forums have different rules, so do read the guidelines before you post for the first time. Here is a general guide to good manners online.

- **Check whether your topic** has already been covered before starting a new discussion (known as a 'thread'). Consider whether your comment is better added to an existing thread.

- **Read all the comments in a thread** before posting your opinion – it may be that someone made the same point earlier on.

- **Don't post the same comment** into multiple threads.

- **Keep on the subject** – it is considered rude to hijack a thread to talk about something else or to have a 'private' conversation with another member.

- **Be civil**. It's easy to dash off a rude riposte but online battles can turn ugly and may result in your being removed by the site's moderators. There is usually a button that you can click to report a user who posts offensive comments.

- **If you have been insulted,** report the fact rather than respond to the person who offended you.

- **Be aware of trolls** – these are people who intend to cause upset, or make up stories in order to get attention. If you think someone is a troll, report the person to the moderators rather than getting angry or challenging him or her.

- **Do not promote your business** or post an advertisement in a discussion thread.

- **Learn the lingo**. Lots of forums use acronyms. There is usually a section that explains these – if you can't find it, type 'acronyms' into the site's search option; see our guide to the most common ones on page 161.

I've found a forum I like. How do I sign up?

Go to the forum's main (home) page, and look for a link saying **Register** or **Sign up**. Click on it and check that you are happy with the site's rules. You will normally have to choose a username and password, provide your email address and give a few personal details, such as your name, date of birth and location. Make sure that these will be kept private from other users before giving this information.

What username should I choose?

You should use a pseudonym on online forums because you are engaging with people you don't know. So make your username short and memorable, without any identifying words – don't choose dadofclara or pedromelbourne, for example.

Now what?

You will usually be sent an email containing a link; you need to click on this to complete your registration (this is so the site can be sure that the email address you have provided actually belongs to you). Once you have done that, you can add comments to ongoing discussions (called 'threads') or start a new one. Some sites encourage you to introduce yourself to other members and have a dedicated section for this purpose.

I have been using the site for a while and someone has suggested meeting up. Is that a good idea?

It can be. Many people develop real-life friendships that started online. But, of course, the way someone presents him- or herself on a forum may be very different than the way he or she is in real life. You should treat any suggestion to meet up with caution and take steps to protect yourself until you get to know another user well – just as you would in online dating (see page 165 for essential safety advice).

Understand acronyms

These acronyms are used in chat rooms, online forums, social networks and in instant messaging and texting.

AFAIK As far as I know

AFK Away from keyboard

ASL Age, sex, location

ATM At the moment

BAK Back at keyboard

BOT Back on topic

BTW By the way

CTN Can't talk now

DH, DW, DS, DD, DM, DF Denotes husband, wife, son, daughter, mother, father and so on. The D stands for dear, or darling.

FTF Face to face

FWIW For what it's worth

HTH Hope that helps

IMO/IMHO In my opinion/In my humble opinion

IYKWIM/IYSWIM If you know what I mean/If you see what I mean

LOL Laugh out loud

NP No problem

OT Off topic

OTT Over the top

PM Private message; many sites allow you to message individual users. Some sites call this DM (direct message).

POV Point of view

RBTL Read between the lines

RL Real life (**IRL** is 'in real life')

ROFL Rolling on floor laughing

RT Realtime, or retweet

RTM Read the manual

TBH To be honest

TIA Thanks in advance

TTYL Talk to you later

TYVM Thank you very much

WYWH Wish you were here

XOXO Hugs and kisses

YY Yes, yes

Emoticons – representations of facial expressions formed by keyboard characters – are another shortcut used online. These are the most common ones, but there are lots of variations.

:) smiling

;) winking

:(frowning

:-D laughing

:'-(crying

:P sticking out tongue

>:O shock (open-mouthed) or yawn

DATING SITES

People keep telling me to try internet dating but I have no idea which site I should go to.

There are hundreds of sites matching potential dates. Narrow down your options by asking for a recommendation. Or look for a site that focuses on a specific group or interest – there are dating sites for sports-lovers, for example, or for people aged over 50. If you read a daily newspaper that runs a dating site, then that can be a good bet – because other people using it are likely to have a similar outlook.

Whichever site you choose, make sure that it has stringent rules against inappropriate behaviour, and that it allows you to message through the site without revealing your email address. It's essential to think about your safety from the outset when using online dating.

Is online dating free?

Some sites are – and they tend to be the most popular ones. Others require you to pay a subscription.

Why would I bother to pay if I can join a free site?

Various reasons. For one, anyone can sign up to a free site so some members may not be serious about meeting new people – there may be profiles set up as a joke or as an advertisement, say. And a paid site will take credit card numbers, which provides a check on users' identities (an important security measure).

How does online dating work?

Some sites let you browse pictures and brief biographies of current users, without becoming a member yourself, though you will need to register in order to make contact. Others let you see other users only once you register (this helps preserve anonymity, so might be a consideration when choosing the right site). Once you have signed up, the site will make suggestions about good matches for you, based on the information that you provide when you sign up.

What information do I have to give about myself, then?

In order to sign up, you'll have to provide some basic details about yourself, some information about the type of person you are looking to meet (his or her age, gender and rough geographical location) and an email address that the site's administrators can use to contact you. Once you are registered, you will be asked to answer lots more questions (your likes and dislikes and so on) and to create a more detailed 'profile' that can be accessed by potential contacts.

The site will make suggestions about good matches for you, based on the information that you provide.

Don't put any identifying information – your address, your place of work, your surname or phone number – into your profile.

How do I write a good profile?

Start with an eye-catching headline that says something about who you are without revealing too much… you want people to read on ('Need a partner for the ice rink' or 'Plays bad guitar, but cooks great pasta', for example, or perhaps use a favourite quote). Think about what makes you unique: a profile should be honest, positive and specific. Rather than saying 'I love cooking or watching films', say 'I love cooking for my friends – especially Thai streetfood…' or 'I adore black and white films from the 50s'. These are the kind of details that may appeal to someone like you.

It's a good idea to write your profile offline rather than directly into the site so that you can leave it a day or so before re-reading it. Double-check the spelling and grammar before you post it.

Do I have to add a photo?

You definitely should. Most people will be keenly interested in what you look like, and you will have a much better response rate if you make a picture available – and often users can choose to browse only those profiles that include one. Choose one in which you look your best, and make it a fairly recent headshot (not a snap of you sitting in your friend's Ferrari ten years ago).

What happens next?

The site will suggest 'matches' for you, based on the information that you and other users have provided. You can browse other members' profiles, and get in touch via the site if you like what they say, and they may contact you. It's a good idea to stick to people who live near you: there's little point in striking up an online friendship with someone who lives 500 kilometres away.

If all goes well, speak on the phone before you meet – a phone call will help you assess whether you want to go ahead. Keep a first meeting short – a cup of coffee or quick lunch is ideal – in case you don't get on as well as you hoped. Always follow the safety guidelines: there are risks to meeting people online, so it is essential to protect yourself.

Staying safe

Personal security on an internet dating site is much like safety on the road – a matter of exercising common sense, and of not proceeding unless you are sure it is safe to do so. Here are a few tips and a few road rules to help you along that romantic highway.

- **Keep personal details out of your username** – Maria_Brasilia or JohnJones_Colchester are bad choices.
- **Don't email for too long before meeting up** – it's easy to start thinking that you know somebody well and let your guard down – in reality until you meet, you cannot know the person is who he or she says.
- **Make sure that your phone number is blocked** when you call someone from a dating (or other online) site.
- **Meet in a public place** where there are lots of people, and stay there.
- **Do make your own way** there and back – don't accept a lift.
- **Tell a friend or family member where you are going,** who you are meeting and when you will be back.
- **Take a mobile phone with you**, and keep it switched on in case you need to make contact with a friend or relative.
- **Never tell anyone your address** or your place of work until you know him or her well enough to feel comfortable – be cautious.
- **Don't leave your personal belongings** or your drink unattended in case of theft or tampering (your drink could be 'spiked' with a drug).
- **Trust your instincts:** if you feel uncomfortable for any reason, leave.

5

NEWS AND KNOWLEDGE

Starting points

- **You can find out pretty much any fact on the internet** – no matter how obscure – by using a search engine.
- **Online resources include** encyclopedias, dictionaries, databases and even entire library collections, which are searchable in just a few clicks.
- **You can watch talks by lecturers** at some of the world's leading universities, for free.
- **Thousands of newspapers are published online** for free: more people now rely on online newspapers than print ones for their daily news.
- **Health websites** are increasingly popular – around a quarter of all Australians regularly look up health and medical information online.

KEY ACTIONS

- Keep up to date with breaking news from around the globe.
- Subscribe to magazines online, and organise your subscriptions.
- Find out about the latest scientific research.
- Access helpful health advice and resources.
- Get customised weather forecasts at home and abroad.
- Learn a language online.

FACT FINDING

Say I just want to check a fact, such as the population of Hungary. Where's the best place to start?

No matter what topic you are looking for information about, one of the first search results you'll encounter will probably be from Wikipedia. This is an online encyclopedia with millions of articles. It is available in more than 270 languages. Wikipedia's articles are written by tens of thousands of volunteer contributors from all over the world – anyone who has access to the internet can write for the site or make changes to existing articles. The broad, collaborative nature of Wikipedia means that vast amounts of information can be found there. There are articles on almost any subject you can think of – from toupees to the Argentine constitution of 1826. All the articles contain hyperlinks (words, phrases or images that you click on to jump to another web page), making it easy to explore related subjects.

If anyone can write for Wikipedia, how can I be sure that the information is reliable?

When Wikipedia first started, its trustworthiness was often called into question. But today's Wikipedia is in fact remarkably reliable, and has been for some time. A 2005 study that compared Wikipedia with the best printed encyclopedias found a similar (very low) level of errors. The fact is that many of Wikipedia's contributors are experts in their own specific field, and they take pride in getting things right. And there are editorial checks and balances in place.

What kind of checks are there?

The site is constantly monitored by Wikipedia's professional editors and by volunteers. Certain high-profile or contentious articles, such as those on international political figures or government organisations, are protected and cannot be edited by public users. In all articles, sources have to be cited – and many of these sources can be reached directly via a hyperlink.

So I can trust the information?

Usually yes, though if you want to use a fact that you have found on Wikipedia, it's a good idea to check it elsewhere – but that goes for any written information, online or not. You'll find a list of sources at the end of articles, which is useful for cross-referencing what you have read. It is always a good idea to go to the first-hand source if you want to check a fact – it is all too easy for someone to manipulate the information or to get it slightly wrong. Of course, you will need to evaluate the first-hand source as well.

How do I evaluate a website?

Here's a good test: copy a short chunk of the text, one that contains a distinctive turn of phrase that is not a quotation, and paste it into a search engine. If the results turn up lots of sites using precisely the same text, this implies that the website obtained its information from some other source – possibly Wikipedia. The information may not be wrong – but if it has been copied from elsewhere then it has probably not been checked by the person who created the site. You can usually conclude that the writer does not know enough about the subject to generate his or her own material.

Here are some other important things to consider when assessing information from a website:

1. If the cut-and-paste test suggests that the website text is original, take a closer look at the words. Is the writing grammatically correct? Are there obvious spelling mistakes? Does the information seem knowledgeable, even-handed and well organised, or patchy, one-sided and slapdash? If the writing is bad in any way, or if the writer seems to have an axe to grind, then the facts may well be dubious, too.

2. Is the owner of the website identified? There should be a 'Contact us' or 'About us' page that contains the name and physical address (rather than simply the email address) of the organisation or person behind it.

3. Who is the author of the information? Is it someone who has professional credentials or – otherwise – does he or she have relevant experience? You need to know the author's perspective in order to assess his or her reliability. Check the name of the person or institution (however official it may sound) by googling it. If it is trustworthy, you would expect to find references to work by that author having appeared in reputable publications elsewhere. You would also expect the institution to be cited as an authority in places other than its own site, or linked sites.

4. Does the author offer evidence for his or her views? Are these legitimate scientific studies that you can verify, for example, or are they simply personal stories, which may not be relevant?

Facts at your fingertips

One of the great things about the internet is that it makes it easy to find facts quickly. Questions that would once have necessitated a trip to the library, and time spent rifling through the indexes of books, can now be answered in seconds. Here are some useful sources for hard facts about the world.

United Nations

If you are looking for hard data on international relations, detailed maps or the dates of national holidays, the official UN website (un.org) has a wealth of resources that you can search.

The World Factbook

An extensive reference resource compiled by the US Central Intelligence Agency (cia.gov), which contains information at a glance about the history, geography, government, economy and people of every country of the world. If you need to know the name of the prime minister of Uzbekistan, the population of Honduras, or which countries share a border with Switzerland, this is a good place to look.

World Leaders

The World Leaders directory (officially called Chiefs of State and Cabinet Members of Foreign Governments) is another resource compiled by the CIA. It lists the names of the heads of state and government members of each country of the world. It is updated on a weekly basis to ensure that all information contained is current, and is a handy place for checking exactly what role an individual whose name you frequently see cropping up in news reports actually holds.

Encyclopedia Britannica

The highly respected encyclopedia (britannica.com) continues to be a valuable source of knowledge, and has been translated into several languages. It is written and maintained by a team of expert contributors and full-time editors. It is now available in an online version on a subscription-only basis, and also as an app that can be downloaded to your mobile device.

NEWS AND SPORTS

I can see that Wikipedia is good for encyclopedic facts. But where do I go for current affairs and breaking news?

There are various ways to keep yourself informed about world events using the internet. It can gather together many of the sources that you would turn to in the 'real' world. All newspapers and broadcasters have websites and apps that – because they are so quick to update – are often the first place they publish headlines, news reports and footage of the latest top stories. You'll be able to find up-to-the-minute information on local, national and global current affairs, entertainment news and sports results. You can also use a search engine to bring up the latest news headlines from around the world and look for stories that interest you.

Tell me more about using a search engine to find out the news.

One simple way of seeing the day's leading news headlines is via a search engine. Google, Yahoo! and Bing, for example, bring together all the top stories from a variety of reputable sources, such as global newspapers and the websites of broadcasters. To find this, go to the home page of your search engine and choose **News** (this might be a tab at the top of your screen or a link on the left-hand side of the page). This brings up a page full of news headlines for you to browse.

I want to find the latest news on a particular subject.

In that case, type your keywords into the search box – 'Chinese economy', for example – and then click on **News**. The search engine will trawl through news websites or the entire internet for the latest stories related to that subject.

All newspapers and broadcasters have websites and apps that are often the first place they publish headlines.

You mentioned newspapers. Are they published online in their entirety?

Most newspapers have their own website and/or app that you can access from your smartphone or tablet. On those sites you'll often be able to see much the same content that you'd find by flicking through the pages of a newspaper – though some newspapers choose to restrict that content, or make it chargeable, so as not to undermine sales of the print version. But in some senses you get more if you turn to the online version of a news publication. For example, many papers and individual journalists have a Twitter account (see page 146) that they use to disseminate details of developing news stories.

Why pay for content?

So much information is available for free on the web that you might think it a waste of money to pay for access to a site. But there are reasons that, in some instances, it might be worth your while.

Imagine that you are a newsagent. You have one customer who comes to the shop every day, picks a newspaper from the pile, reads it from cover to cover, then replaces it and leaves the shop without a word. If you were that newsagent, sooner or later you would be bound to tell the customer to stop doing it, that if he wants to read a paper, then he should buy one and take it away. If your favourite news provider announces that it is going to start charging readers to access its content, then it's up to you to decide whether you are prepared to pay. There are some questions you might like to ask yourself:

- **Can I get the same information for free elsewhere?** For example, if it is sports news you are after, are there other sites that provide the same breadth of information, and that you could enjoy just as much? If so, you might as well change your allegiance and save the money.

- **If you regularly buy the print version of the publication in question,** would you theoretically be happy to switch entirely to the digital version? Or would you miss the rustle of your morning paper?

- **If you are happy to read your paper online,** how many times a week or year would you have to buy the print version to equal the cost of an online subscription? If you buy the paper only once or twice a week, a subscription may not be economical.

- **Would the online version of your paper suit the way you use it**? Do you read your paper on the train? (If so, you may have to factor in the additional expense of a laptop or tablet unless you already have one.) Do you, say, like to do the crossword? (You might find it's not quite the same when you have to fill in the answers on screen.)

- **Are there aspects of reading your favourite newspaper online** that may be a boon to you, even if you have to pay for the privilege? Say, for example, you have trouble with your eyesight. You could benefit from 'accessibility' features that are built into your computer, such as the ability to increase the size of type.

Can I access TV news online?

Yes, you can. The websites of the many available news broadcasters are a great place to start. Channels such as the ABC, BBC, Sky News, CNN, and Euronews all offer comprehensive international news coverage, with text-based articles complemented by audio interviews and video reports. There are also online-only news sites such as The Huffington Post. To view the video news broadcast or listen to the audio clip, click or press the **Play** button – usually a right-pointing triangle ▶ – and the clip will launch in your browser.

Where's the best place to look for reliable international news headlines?

If you are looking for information from a particular country, you can try searching for the website of that country's official news agency or press agency. High-profile news agencies that operate multinationally and have a leading reputation for quality news coverage include Reuters, Agence France-Presse and Associated Press. If the official news agency is likely to be less than reliable – as is usually the case in non-democratic regimes – then you will often find that there are non-government news agencies, websites, online newspapers and bloggers that you can access.

Can I subscribe to magazines online?

Many magazines offer an online version, which contains pretty much the same content as the paper version. Some of these online magazines are sold on a subscription basis. You can download a sample of each month's issue for free, but you pay a monthly subscription or one-off fee to be able to access the full edition. Many magazines publish digital content in a version specially designed for tablet and smartphone users. These are designed to look good on a smaller screen, and they will often contain interactive content: video footage of the editor by way of an introduction, links to previously published articles on the same topic or direct links to online stores, say.

International news and comment is just a click away – you can get it from the official press agency, online newspapers or individual bloggers.

All about blogs

The internet has made it possible for all kinds of people to share and publish information. Now anyone can set up a website and make known their knowledge, opinions and feelings about a particular subject, or about life in general. Blogs (short for 'web logs') are online journals that contain regular updates (similar to diary entries, but written to be read immediately by others). They are usually the work of a single person, but a blog can also be a group activity.

Blogs vary massively in ambition and quality. The best political sites, for example, are almost like newspapers. Some bloggers use the medium to bypass state censors in oppressive countries, or to draw attention to a particular cause. But most blogs are an expression of the blogger's daily life or less urgent concerns or are an outlet for a hobby or leisure interest.

All bloggers, whatever their theme, want readers, and so they encourage people to sign up to receive the updates, and to post comments below the blog post. There may be videos and images as well as articles, and you can usually search old blog posts as well as the most recent ones. A blog that consists entirely or mostly of video is termed a 'vlog'. Most blogs links to other blogs or websites with similar themes – so they are a way of keeping up with what people are saying or thinking on a particular subject.

Popular blogging services include WordPress, Tumblr and Blogger. You can use these websites to find bloggers that you are interested in, or to set up a blog of your own for free.

How do I get the online version of a magazine?

If you're using an iPhone or an iPad, you will already have the Apple Newsstand app, which is a kind of virtual newsagent. Open the app, and touch the **Store** button. You will be taken to a page where you can download the sample version of any magazine that is on sale. Once downloaded, each magazine or newspaper is displayed as an icon on the app's 'virtual bookshelves'. The front cover of the latest edition of each magazine will automatically be shown, and a notification alerts you whenever a new issue is published and new content is available. To get the whole edition, you tap on the cover, and proceed as if you were buying a new app (see page 198 for advice on how to do this).

If you have an Android device, then you will find Newsstand in the Google Play Store, which works in a similar way. Next Issue, available on Windows 8 smartphones and tablets, as well as on iPhones, iPads and Android devices, is another app that helps you to find, download and manage subscription content.

What about sports? Can I find the latest results online?

You certainly can. Just as with the latest news headlines, you'll be able to find up-to-the minute sports news online, including live text commentary and video footage. Services such as Yahoo! Sports, BBC Sport and ESPN ScoreCenter mean that you will never miss a goal, run or race – and you'll be able to watch video footage of game highlights (and in some cases watch the event live).

Where's the best place to find other sports information?

As well as current news stories and the latest fixtures and results, the official web page of a sport's governing body or a major competition – such as the NRL, FIFA, the ATP World Tour or the International Olympic Committee – usually provides a comprehensive resource on anything you could ever want to know about that sport, including archives of previous news headlines and features, historical records and results, and photo and video galleries of past competitions and events.

Most sports teams – from Brazil's Santos FC and the New York Yankees baseball team to your local cricket club – now have their own websites and Twitter accounts where you can keep up to date.

I want to know the news as soon as it happens. How can I keep up to date?

Many news sites offer a handy service called RSS (which stands for 'Really Simple Syndication'). If you use RSS, websites can deliver their latest news updates (in the form of simple headlines) directly to your computer – without your having to check the sites yourself. You will need an RSS reader to do it: this will regularly scan all your chosen sites for new content and then display it for you, all together in one place. You may already be using a type of RSS reader if you have a personalised home page (such as My Yahoo! or My MSN) – this is how you get news, weather and other updates on your page. Some browsers have a built-in feed reader: this is called Live Bookmarks on Firefox and RSS Feeds on Internet Explorer; others require you to download a feed reader as an add-on from your browser's online store (see page 72 for information about using add-ons). And some email programs also offer the facility to have feeds delivered to your inbox.

How do I choose my feeds?

It works like this: if you want to be kept updated with the latest *Sydney Morning Herald* headlines, say, go to the website of the *Sydney Morning Herald* and find the page with links to the different RSS channels. Click on the area that interests you, and you'll be taken to a page with an RSS icon where you can choose how you want to subscribe – that is, whether you want the updates to go to your Yahoo! page or to Live Bookmarks, for example. Repeat this process for any other type of news story, or updates from any website that you'd like to receive regularly. Then go to your RSS feed reader and you'll be able to access all your chosen web feeds instantly – and together. Alternatively, you can sign up to an online feed reader and read your feeds on its website. Or you can download its app to your mobile device – Feedly is one such service. You search for sites or stories of interest to you through the site/app, and add them to your page, where they are displayed, magazine-style, with images.

BOOKS AND LITERATURE

Can I read books online as well as magazines and newspapers?

This is another amazing thing about the internet: it gives you instant access to millions of books. The net makes it easy to buy them new – just like any other commodity – from an online store (see page 261). And a simple search makes it possible to track down bibliographic rarities or obscure books to any second-hand bookstore that keeps an online catalogue of its stock (as many now do). You can do what was once impossible: scan miles of dusty shelving around the world in a couple of clicks.

But the internet has brought about a much more far-reaching shift in the way we use books. E-books – texts that are bought, delivered and read in digital form – have changed the way that we read books. Almost every new novel – and many non-fiction works – are now published as e-books as well as in traditional paper form. The e-book is usually significantly cheaper than the paper version, because there are no print costs.

The internet gives you instant access to millions of books – from much-loved classics to brand-new bestsellers.

What's the best way to read an e-book?

The most comfortable way is on an e-reader, which is a light, hand-held internet device designed to be as portable and legible as a print-on-paper version (see page 182). You can change the size of the type (and the font) to suit yourself. Lots of people read books on a tablet – which has the advantage of being able to display colour images, so is better for illustrated books. You can also read e-books on a smartphone (though you may find the print uncomfortably small) or on the screen of a desktop or laptop computer. You may need to download a book-reading app – Amazon offers a free Kindle app for most devices – or this may be built in.

I have just bought an e-reader. How do I start building a digital book collection?

You will need to give a method of payment when you set up your e-reader – you only have to do this once. Somewhere on the e-reader's home screen there will be an icon for the online store. Tap on this, type the name of the book you want into the search bar or browse through the various menus to check books on offer. Tap on the book's title, and then tap the **Buy** button, and it will download onto your device straight away (you may have to type in your password). You can also opt to download a sample – a chapter or two. When you reach the end, you get the option to buy the whole book. A tablet works in exactly the same way.

How about free books? Is there anywhere I can get those?

You can, but not all books. Books that are out of copyright (usually because the author is long dead) are often available in online versions for free. Books that are in copyright have to be paid for, so that the writer or his estate continues to receive a royalty.

Project Gutenberg (gutenberg.org) is a voluntary project that offers an impressive online collection of more than 40,000 full versions of books. Many classic titles can be found there, including the works of authors such as William Shakespeare, Jane Austen and Charles Dickens. You don't need to register to search the database of titles. If you're unsure where to start, look at the site's list of its Top 100 Books, where you'll see the titles that are the most popular with other readers. You can choose to read these e-books for free, or to download them to your computer or mobile device. All the main online bookstores – including Amazon, iTunes and Google Play – also offer free, out-of-copyright titles for downloading, although you may still need to register a payment method in order to do this.

Should I buy an e-reader?

You can read books on a tablet or even a smartphone, but many people prefer to have a dedicated e-book reader (an e-reader), which is smaller and weighs less than a tablet, so is much easier to hold. E-readers have a better reading screen, too: it is a lot easier on the eyes than the screen of a tablet because there is no glare, and it can be read in bright sunlight. An e-reader can store hundreds of books at once, so it is essentially a mobile library. It is particularly handy if you commute or for holidays, and has a much longer battery life than a tablet.

There are various e-readers available, including Amazon's Kindle, the Kobo Arc and the Nook. Some e-readers have a back-light built in for reading in the dark, such as the Kindle Paperwhite, the Kobo Glo and the Nook Simple Touch.

ACADEMIC RESOURCES

What about academic journals? Can I access them online?

One of the boons of the internet age is that academic writing has become much more accessible. The largest online academic resource is JSTOR, which offers digitised versions of more than 2000 journals, periodicals and research articles. At the moment, the main collection can't be accessed by private individuals, but if you are affiliated to an academic institution, public library, research institution, museum or school that has an active subscription, you may be able to gain access to the collections.

How do I track down academic articles?

Google Scholar is a free service that allows users to search for keywords in academic resources, including journals, technical reports and research theses. Go to scholar.google.com.au (or use your country's suffix). Enter your keyword in the search box, and you'll be provided with a list of search results that are sorted in order of relevance to your keyword. Many of the results you see will require you to subscribe to the publishing website of the journal or article before you can read the full text but short extracts should be available.

Sounds brilliant. What other academic resources are available online?

Top universities from around the globe, including Harvard, Berkeley, Oxford and Cambridge, regularly make lectures on a range of academic subjects available for free on their websites. University College London offers live streams of some of its lectures, as well as video podcasts.

Museum websites can also be a good resource for quality academic research – the online collections of the Smithsonian have more than 8 million digital records that can be accessed, while more than 2 million digital records exist in the British Museum's collection, and around 2000 new image records are being added each week. The UK's Open University – which specialises in distance learning – has made a selection of lectures available for free on its YouTube site (see page 226 for more about YouTube). Free learning resources are available from its OpenLearn site and you can try out a range of short introductory courses – also for free.

So I have to go to each website to try and find a lecture I am interested in?

There are some general resources. The website academicearth.org has collected together links to various lectures from some of the world's leading institutions, including Harvard, Yale, Princeton, Oxford and the Indian Institute of Technology.

If you're just looking for thought-provoking commentary, have a look through the BBC's archive of Reith Lectures, which includes every lecture ever broadcast since the series' inauguration in 1948. And check out the iTunes U app, which enables users to download a selection of lectures and talks from celebrated academics from more than 400 universities around the world. You can access these audio and video files for free on your home PC or Mac, or install the iTunes U app if you have an iPad or iPhone.

HEALTH AND MEDICAL

What kind of health and medical issues can I find out about online?

Pretty much any issue. No matter how unusual the ailment or condition, the chances are that someone has written about it online or designed an app that will help you to find out the facts you need. The most commonly researched health topics are specific diseases or conditions, symptoms, treatments or procedures. People also search for information on particular hospitals, doctors or other healthcare professionals.

What apps are available?

All sorts. There are apps such as WebMD that allow you to input symptoms and receive a (tentative) diagnosis; there are others that give first-aid advice or treatment tips or allow you to track your symptoms.

There are even guides that identify drugs and medicines by pill-shape and colour (for example, Pill Identifier).

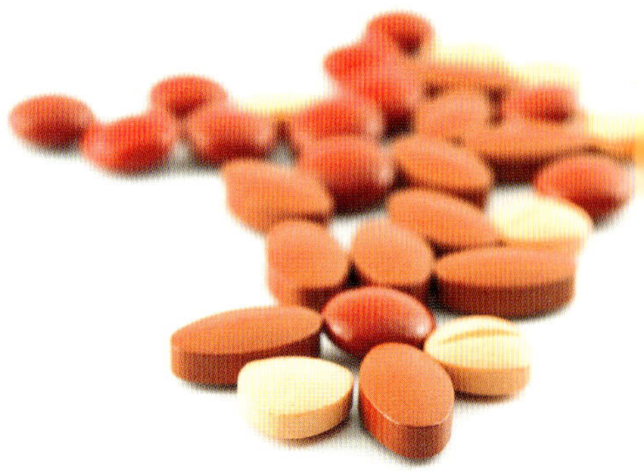

There is no substitute for visiting your GP and getting professional advice when you really need it.

As good as going to the doctor, then?

Well, no, not really. There is no substitute for visiting your GP and getting professional advice when you really need it. Don't fall into the trap of diagnosing yourself (or your family members) with every ailment, bug and epidemic just because you read something online that sounds a bit similar to your symptoms. There's definitely some good information out there – health professionals use the web to track down the latest research – but you need to learn how to understand it. You always need to exercise caution when researching facts on the internet and this is doubly important when you are looking at health.

Can the web help me to find a doctor in my area?

Yes, there are lots of ways the web can help you to find a doctor. For a start, there are websites that list general practitioners in pretty much any city or area. To find these, simply type 'find a doctor' plus the name of the city/area you are in. These directories can be very useful – not only for finding a doctor in your home town, but also when you are on holiday or travelling for business. There are websites that offer ratings on doctors, but most healthcare professionals do not think that these offer a helpful assessment of a doctor's skill.

The web is a useful tool if you are looking for a specialist – if you want to see a dermatologist, for example, then you can type in 'doctor, dermatology' plus your city (or the nearest one). The results will include the websites of doctors and clinics, with details of services, location and other useful patient information. Before visiting any doctor you find on the net, it is a good idea to go to the website of the governing medical body for the country you are in – and check that he or she is registered. You can also type the doctor's name and specialisation into a search engine to see what academic papers he or she has published. This can give you an idea of his or her standing.

There are also websites where you can pose a medical question and get an answer from a qualified doctor – askthedoctor.com is one. The advice is general in nature, but can be a good way of getting information. You can look through thousands of previous questions and answers, too.

Health sites that count...

If you are looking for health information on the internet:

- **Start with official websites**, which offer up-to-date, well-researched information on symptoms and treatments, as well as details about clinical trials. Try the US National Institute of Health (nih.gov, which receives 20 million visitors a month), the UK's NHS Choices website (nhs.uk), the World Health Organization (who.int) and the Victorian State Government's Better Health Channel (betterhealth.vic.gov.au). Sites that end in .gov should be reliable because only government organisations can use this suffix – at least you know the sites are reputable and that the information is likely to have been rigorously researched.

- **You should also look at sites belonging to educational institutions** (they have the suffix .edu). These can be a great source of research-based information. But do bear in mind that some institutions are allied with particular health companies and the research may be skewed in their favour.

- **Another good bet are associations, charities and other non-profit organisations** (these sites are designated .org). These, too, often provide links to new research, and may also run helplines and other services. National charities can be the most helpful because they can help you pinpoint treatment options where you live; however, American sites (heart.org, for example) tend to be well funded and have strong research links. Be aware that anyone can obtain a .org suffix, so you need to check the site is run by a reputable organisation.

- **Don't discount commercial sites** – some have become highly respected for the sound, comprehensive advice they provide. The WebMD, Mayo Clinic, medicinenet.com and drugs.com websites are all popular and worthwhile. But, of course, there are many .com health websites that exist purely to promote certain products, so you need to exercise caution.

- **If you are looking for the latest cutting-edge research**, search for websites belonging to universities and other educational institutions (make sure they are bona fide), where you can access the latest research papers and articles. The NIH maintains a useful and free database of research (called PubMed) that you can access.

And those that don't...

Be wary of:

- **Sites overloaded with advertisements**, or promising miracle cures.

- **Sites that push** a particular treatment option or remedy, whether they are commercial or alternative.

- **Personal blogs** – these can be interesting reading, and can contain good information, but one person's subjective experience will not necessarily tell you anything about your own health.

6

THE PRACTICAL WEB

Starting points

- **The internet is not just** a library and a shopping mall, it is also a resource you can use for fun and entertainment: a kind of theatre and a playground.
- **You'll be able** to find advice, information and tutorials on any hobby or leisure pastime imaginable – from taking pictures to playing an instrument.
- **You can store** your photographs online – about 500 million photos are uploaded every day – and share them with people you know, and people you don't.
- **The internet has changed** the way we plan our holidays – you can now research and book your own travel rather than relying on an agent. More than half of all travel reservations are now made online.

KEY ACTIONS

- Print, edit and share your photos online.
- Play games – on your own or against opponents.
- Download apps to your mobile device.
- Get up-to-date weather and traffic news.
- Find the best hotel deals and book bargain flights.
- Troubleshoot problems with your computer, your home, your life.

PHOTOGRAPHY

I've always taken my photographs to be printed at a shop. What's the best way to do it online?

There are many online photo-printing services that allow you to upload pictures from your computer, tablet or smartphone to a website. From there, you can order copies of your photos in a range of sizes and pay for them securely with a debit or credit card. And they offer more than the old-fashioned set of prints. You can easily turn your pictures into photo books, greeting cards, mouse mats, mugs, jigsaw puzzles, fridge magnets, calendars and more: if you can put a photo on it, you'll find a website willing to help you create it. You order online, and the items are sent to you in the post.

The photo website asked for access to my computer – is it safe to allow this?

If you're uploading photos to an online photo-ordering website from your laptop or computer, the site might require you to install special software that allows the site to access your machine to copy your files. If it is a reputable service, this should be fine, but it's always wise to ensure that you have up-to-date virus protection on your machine before you agree to install any new software.

A friend tells me I should be storing my photos online. Is that really the case?

It's a good idea to do this. For a start, it saves using up space on your computer and it means that you will always have your pictures – even if something goes wrong with your device. An online photo-sharing website will let you store photos for free. Popular sites include Flickr, Shutterfly and Instagram. You can also store photos on Facebook and Google+. Storing your photos online saves space on your computer, and there is an added benefit in that it amounts to a back-up copy of all your pictures. So if you lose your tablet or your computer seizes up, at least you don't lose your pictures, too. You'll still be able to access all the photos you've uploaded to the photo-storage site from a different device.

So, how does sharing work? Can I limit who can see my pictures?

It is easy to set up access to photo-sharing websites, and make it possible for your pictures to reach audiences as large or as small as you like. Users can change the privacy settings on the photos they upload to allow content to be made public, visible to family, visible to friends or private (so that they are the only ones allowed access).

I'm worried where pictures I put on Facebook or Google+ might end up. Is that paranoid?

Not really. It's a fact that once you share something online, you cannot control what happens to it. For a start, one of the people you share your photographs with could copy them to another computer, or put them on a social-networking page, where they will be seen by his or her own contacts, and so on. In the end, you have to think carefully about what you are comfortable with, and make decisions accordingly.

What can I do to ensure that my photos stay private?

If you don't want there to be any chance of your photos somehow slipping through the privacy net and into the public domain, then stick to a zero-risk option and either don't put them online in any shape or form or change the settings on the site you are using so that the images are visible only to you. If you want to share photographs, then be sure to read and understand the site's terms of service before you do so. Make sure that you change the privacy settings rather than leaving them as the default option (which may allow anyone to view your images). And never, ever upload anything that you consider very private.

It's good to share

More than half of people taking snaps post them online for others to enjoy. You can do this via a social network – or you can use a photo-sharing website or app. Here are four popular ways to share your images.

Instagram

This app allows you to take photographs with your mobile phone and then apply a filter and frame to create a more memorable image that you share on your Instagram account (and on various social-media sites too, if you like). Anyone can see or comment on your images unless you change the settings to private, which means you have to approve people first. You can also share videos.

Snapchat

Users of this app send smartphone images as messages to other users (like texting) but the image can be viewed for only a few moments before it disappears – it's a fun way of sharing snaps without allowing others to keep them or send them on.

Flickr

With Flickr you upload photos from a computer or mobile device, and organise them into sets. You control who your photos are shared with and can change the audience for specific photos. You get a whole terabyte of free storage – that's around 500,000 photos. You can also order prints and create photobooks and other items on the site. You need a Yahoo!, Facebook or Google account to sign up.

Shutterfly

This is a photo-printing site where you create an online website. Your site gets its own web address that you share with friends and family. There's no limit on the number of photos you can add, and you can upload them from any internet device or from social networks.

I've just taken a great picture on my phone. Can I get it onto the web from there, or do I have to transfer it to my computer first?

All smartphones come with the option to share photos online. This can be done immediately after you've taken the photograph, or else by locating the photo later in the phone's photo gallery. Select the photo and tap the [↑] – you'll see a number of options asking you to choose where you want your photo to be posted. These vary depending on the phone you have but include social networks and photo-sharing sites such as Flickr or Picasa (you will need to set up an account, and then sign into it from your phone).

I love sharing my photographs, and want to take better images. Are there any websites that can teach me how?

You may be surprised by the number of good photography tutorials you can access online – for free. The website digital-photography-school.com covers everything from purchasing your next camera to understanding exposure and optimum photography conditions. The in-depth video tutorials help amateur photographers to capture professional shots, and each week an 'assignment topic' is posted, inviting users to submit their own photos. Other popular sites with extensive easy-to-access resources include those of camera manufacturers Nikon, Canon and Sony. You can download the short Photography 101 podcasts, which offer detailed guides on many aspects of photography, if you have an Apple device; you can also watch them on YouTube (see page 226).

And once I have taken my shot, can I edit it online to improve its look?

Photo-editing used to be something that only the professionals did. Nowadays anyone can enhance their images by, say, removing the 'red-eye' that you often get with flash photography, adjusting the brightness or contrast, cropping out objects in the background, applying special effects or adding a border. You can do this on photo-sharing websites and apps as well as dedicated photo-editing sites (fotor.com) or apps (such as Aviary).

HOBBIES AND GAMES

I can see that the internet is a great resource for photographers. What about other hobbies?

No matter what activity you're looking for information about, there's bound be a whole community of like-minded individuals out there, sharing their enthusiasm and exchanging stories, tips and advice. You've just got to know where – and how – to find them.

Where do I start?

Type a keyword into your search engine, one that best describes your hobby: birdwatching, bowling, clock-restoring, postcard-collecting... Have a quick look through the list of search results. However obscure or specialised your hobby is you're bound to come across a mixture of official organisation websites, informal communities of enthusiasts, video clips and tutorials, and links to books and other products of interest. (See also the section on online forums, page 158.)

YouTube (youtube.com) is another handy place to start: whether you have an urge to learn how to play the guitar, paint watercolours, or arrange roses in a vase, there'll be video content that you can learn from: simply type your keywords into the search bar, browse through the results and click on the one that interests you. For more about YouTube, see page 226.

I need some inspiration!

If you just want to see what the web has to offer in terms of hobbies, try visiting discoverahobby.com, which features articles, discussion forums, useful website lists and instructional videos on more than 250 different pastimes, including model-making, ballroom dancing and genealogy. Try clicking on the 'Random hobby' button to see what comes up.

No matter what activity you're looking for information about, there's bound be a whole community of like-minded individuals out there.

My hobby is chess – is it possible to play a game online?

Certainly. If you don't have a nearby opponent to provide you with a challenge, the internet can pair you up with a partner to match your skill level – chess.com is one free site; it also has an app you can download to your phone or tablet.

The same goes for many other games of skill and intellect. If you find yourself wide awake at 3am and fancy passing the time with a game of Scrabble, the internet can provide you with an opponent within minutes. Whether you like card games, word games, trivia quizzes, jigsaw puzzles, arcade games, driving, shooting or ball games or different kinds of puzzles – you'll be able to find what you're looking for online.

If you don't have a nearby opponent to provide you with a challenge, the internet can pair you up with a partner to match your skill level.

How about bridge? For that you need a partner plus two opponents.

No problem. There is always a game you can join, and it does away with the need to arrange an evening of it (though of course online bridge is not quite the same from a socialising point of view). Some bridge websites require you to install software before you can play, while on others you can play directly in your browser. You'll find large bridge communities at OKBridge, Bridge Base Online and FunBridge – these sites (and many others) also have apps, for mobile and tablet users to download and play on the go.

When I play a game online, who am I actually playing against?

Some online chess and bridge games let you play on your own – that is, against 'robots' (by which they mean a computer). If you want a more interactive experience, there are games where you can connect to a network of online players and play against 'real' people. This can be as anonymous as you want it to be, and you'll be identified only by your self-chosen username. Some online games are linked to Facebook, meaning that you can see what games your friends are playing and challenge them or try and beat their scores.

I like challenging crosswords and sudokus. Can I get those online?

You can indeed. Online versions of these are available, too, both in website and app form. The internet contains vast resources of puzzle activities that you can access. Sites such as bestcrosswords.com, onlinecrosswords.net and websudoku.com allow you to complete the puzzles directly in your browser – or, if you prefer, you can print out a paper copy and fill it in the traditional paper way.

What about when I am stuck?

If you are feeling stumped and aren't against accepting a little help, you can use an online crossword solver or anagram generator to see if you can fill in the gaps – just type those phrases into a search engine to find one.

Get the app

Apps are computer programs designed for use on touchscreen devices such as smartphones and tablets. Some come pre-loaded on your device; others you buy, or download for free. Thousands of apps are available, meaning you can customise your device to perform the tasks and functions that you require. If you want to play a game, test your heart rate, tune your guitar, compare prices or listen to the radio, there is an app for it.

Open the store

Every smartphone and tablet comes pre-loaded with an online store for apps – for example, the App Store in Apple devices or Play Store in Android devices. Tap the store icon to open it. You will have to set up an account to use the store the first time you use it and will need to select a payment method (see below).

Find what you want

Click on the search icon – usually a magnifying glass – to search particular keywords (or the name of the app). You can also browse the bestsellers list, look specifically for free or paid-for apps, or search under categories such as Games.

Download it

Tap on the app you want. On the app page that opens you can read the maker's description or check the reviews by other users. If you want to download the app, click **Install**. You may need to input your password before the download starts.

How do I pay?

You can pay by credit card, with gift vouchers (available online or from a shop) or via the online website PayPal (see page 257).

Watch out!

Keep your password private and do not share it with children under any circumstances. It is all too easy to download expensive apps or to pay for extras in gaming apps, and some children have run up huge bills on their parents' accounts in this way. See opposite for how to prevent this.

I want to play a few games to pass the time. Tell me some good sites.

You will find many games on the internet. Most are not educational or improving; they are simply diverting. They range from digital versions of old favourites – card, board and dice games – to puzzles or brainteasers invented for the computer or touchscreen. Try games.com, games.yahoo.com and zone.msn.com for a good selection of these to play on a browser.

How do I play games on my phone?

There are thousands of gaming apps available for mobile devices – and they are among the most popular apps to download. Just visit the online store on your device and look at the bestselling apps, or search the games category. The vast choice includes animated games (many of them with comical graphics), games in which you create a miniature world (such as a farm or town) and absorbing logic games, in which you have to solve increasingly difficult problems as you progress through the levels. They are a fun way to fill an idle five minutes.

Do I have to pay to play?

Many game websites don't require users to pay. If you're downloading game apps to your smartphone or tablet, some are available free of charge (though you usually have to watch ads); others require you to pay a fee before downloading. Some are very cheap, while more sophisticated games can be quite expensive. Once you've paid for the app, you can access the game as much as you want. Be aware that some free games encourage you to purchase some kind of 'virtual' (digital) currency, or to pay a fee for new 'episodes'. The costs can quickly mount up; if children use your device, make sure downloads are protected by a passcode or password that only you know.

How do I set a passcode or password to stop my children paying for apps?

It depends on your device. On Apple devices, go into the general **Settings** menu, then **General**, then **Restrictions** to set a passcode. Make sure **In-App purchases** and **Installing Apps** is set to 'on'. On Android devices, go to Play Store, then **Settings** and **Password (Use password to restrict purchases)**. You'll find similar settings in the Amazon Kindle Fire, and in Windows phones and tablets.

How do I go about playing bingo online?

Bingo is popular on the internet. Many websites have special deals for new players, for example, the incentive of a free deposit to your account when you sign up. Playing bingo on the internet can be fun, but as with any online activity you need to choose a reputable site. Go for a company that you know if possible. Word of mouth – or the internet equivalent, online reviews and feedback communities – is also quite a reliable way to start. Do an internet search for some independent reviews of the bingo site – type its name and the word 'reviews' into a search engine. If you can't find any user reviews of a site/app then it might be one to avoid. As with any website that requires you to enter your card details online, you should check that the page is secure (see page 54) before you enter financial information.

I've found a site. How do I add funds and access any winnings?

Most reputable bingo sites will allow you to add credit to your bingo account using PayPal (see page 257). This secure payment method gives you peace of mind, because the site can never access more money than you give it permission to take, and you don't need to provide the bingo provider with your bank details. You'll be able to withdraw your winnings into your PayPal account and then transfer these to your own bank account. You can also pay using a credit or debit card, and any funds that you win will be transferred to the account you paid with.

Online gambling

For better or worse, the internet has made it much easier to have a flutter. You can bet on the outcome of football matches while you watch the game live, buy lottery tickets and scratch cards, visit virtual casinos and dedicated poker websites. There are hundreds of sites asking you to risk some cash for the chance of a jackpot.

Is it legal?

There are strict rules about how – and where – online gambling websites can operate. Certain countries, including the United States, do not allow gambling websites to be physically located within their borders. Even participating in online gambling is illegal in certain countries. You'll need to check whether the country where you live has restrictions such as these.

Limiting your spending

Many sites offer the ability to set a maximum spend limit, which players can decide upon before they play. When you reach this limit you will be barred from accessing the website for a certain amount of time. This prevents players from overspending in the heat of the moment. It's quite difficult to get around as the limit is linked to your personal details and credit cards.

When gambling becomes addictive

The thrill of gambling creates a natural high that can quickly become addictive. With online gambling, this is particularly true as it is so easily accessible – you can place bets or play from your home computer, mobile device or smartphone, day or night, as long as you have an internet connection (and access to funds to stake). Some people can become addicted to computer games in the same way. If you find yourself becoming preoccupied with gambling or gaming, and spending increasing amounts of time and money on it, then think about seeking help from a support organisation, such as Gamblers Anonymous or GamCare.

HEALTHY LIVING

It's not a hobby exactly – but I'd like some help keeping fit.

If you want to kickstart a healthy new lifestyle, you will find internet resources to help you with every aspect. On YouTube (see page 226) there are lots of circuit-training routines led by professional personal trainers as well as videos showing individual users' amateur exercise regimes for you to follow. Smartphone and tablet users can download apps that help with setting fitness goals.

But my problem is not so much knowing how to exercise as keeping motivated.

The internet can help with that, too. A number of apps and websites have been designed to help you keep track of every aspect of your fitness regime, regardless of what sport or exercise you undertake. Some cater for one specific sport or discipline, while others enable you to monitor your general health and fitness goals, alongside diet and lifestyle patterns.

Sounds good, but I'll need reminding to use the app!

Charting your fitness activities and seeing visual records of your progress towards a goal may be enough motivation to stick to your regime. But for those who need extra encouragement, once you've signed up, fitness apps will send you regular alerts checking up on your progress and reminding you to log in and record your exercise sessions – MapMyFitness or MyFitnessPal are two such apps. You can even find apps that will regularly send you motivational quotes, just in case you feel your focus slipping and need a gentle push in the right direction.

What choices are there for runners?

If you have a smartphone, you can download apps such as MapMyRun, Endomondo or Runkeeper. These use your phone's GPS to track your running data including the duration, distance covered and speed – GPS stands for global positioning system; it means your phone is in touch with a satellite system that tells it exactly where you are, right down to the very spot on a street. When you've finished, you can view the route you followed – or you can use the app to plan your route in advance. They are a great way to keep track of progress and to map out future challenges (say, by constructing a route that is exactly 10km or half-marathon length). Many of these running apps allow you to upload data to the corresponding website, where you can turn the information into a running log, or a graph showing your improvement – because as all runners know, there is nothing more motivating than seeing that you have achieved a new personal best.

What about less intense exercise regimes? Yoga, for example?

It might seem a little odd to practise something as meditative as yoga with your smartphone by your side, but there are apps for yoga as for everything else. Yoga Pro and Pocket Yoga are two that might appeal to you. You can follow virtual yoga sessions that vary in intensity and length, all of them with audio and video instructions.

And there are lots of yoga websites where you can find out more about the practice, too – yogajournal.com is one respected site – and there are plenty of virtual classes on YouTube (see page 226). Many world-renowned yoga teachers have their own websites where you can sign up for newsletters, find details of their workshops and watch demonstrations.

I do lots of different activities – can I track them all together somehow?

Yes. MyFitnessPal and MapMyFitness are among the specially designed health and fitness apps that allow you to track every activity you do (and also everything you eat and drink). You can use the apps in conjunction with the website to keep track of your dietary intake and kilojoules burned – so this is about more than just exercise. Everything you add to the app or website is synched so that your account is always up to date, however you view it. The GymGoal app and website sets you up with a customised workout and lets you record all your exercise sessions with progress charts to show you just how well you are meeting your goals.

What about diet? Are there websites to help me keep to a healthy eating plan?

The internet is awash with diet and weight-loss advice – not all of it good. Steer away from sites promising a magic 'quick fix' or advertisements guaranteeing unrealistic weight loss rates. But online communities are a great way of staying motivated and finding support from others as you aim to slim down. Weight-loss clubs such Jenny Craig, CalorieKing and WeightWatchers have websites (some also have apps) that are designed to keep you motivated. You can subscribe to membership services, access databases of recipes and take part in regular online 'weigh-ins'. Seeing your weekly progress plotted in a spreadsheet may be just the encouragement you need.

Online communities are a great way of staying motivated and finding support from others.

IN THE HOME

I do odd jobs around the house, but I don't always know the right way to go about them. Where can I get tips?

From putting up shelves to changing a fuse or the grim task of unblocking a U-bend, it's safe to say that there is an expert who has shared his or her know-how online. Sites such as diyonline.com and eHow are a great source for all things DIY, with advice ranging from simple tasks (such as changing a light bulb) to ambitious large-scale home restoration projects. YouTube (see page 226) is a good resource if you work well with visual instructions. It has video clips that will take you through all manner of practical tasks, such as changing a bicycle tyre or wiring a plug. The website wikiHow also offers step-by-step guides to a number of household repair and maintenance tasks, with detailed photographs at every stage. As with Wikipedia, anyone can write or edit articles for the website (see page 169 for more about this).

But many of those experts are surely just ordinary people like me?

Some of them, certainly. But as with so much internet-related information, you have to assess the quality of it for yourself. Ask yourself these questions: has the video been shot professionally, or at least carefully? Are the written responses to the video positive and do they ring true? Is the 'expert' sponsored by a trustworthy organisation – say, a brand of tools or a known DIY store?

There are thousands of recipe websites and apps and they allow you to search by ingredient, by course or by name of dish.

Where can I turn for basic cookery tuition?

For reliably good advice, try marthastewart.com, deliaonline.com or thekitchn.com. Or YouTube (see page 226) offers a great many cookery videos that have been uploaded by users, and you can easily browse for a recipe or cooking technique that meets your needs.

I'm bored with the meals I cook. Where can I find some new recipe suggestions?

If you're in need of inspiration for dinner, or maybe have some ingredients in your refrigerator that you need to use up, a quick online search could help. There are thousands of recipe websites and apps that allow you to search by ingredient, by course or by name of dish. Go to readersdigest.com.au and have a look at the food section. Or try the award-winning epicurious.com or its smartphone app – you can browse, search, save and share over 30,000 meal recipes. Another useful website to try is allrecipes.com, where users can explore dishes by cooking method as well as ingredients and occasion.

Three sites that give the answers

Whatever you want to know, you can find the information on the web. Here are some general sites where you can find practical advice, and get answers to specific queries.

About.com This site has thousands of articles on lifestyle topics such as travel, parenting and health. The articles are written and updated by a team of writers. They are arranged by category as well as listed alphabetically according to subject, so it's easy to find what you need. The site covers such matters as how to use up leftovers, do your bit to reduce global warming, or produce a dazzling CV.

eHow.com A kind of manual for life skills such as cookery, money management, DIY and so on. You type in keywords to search a database of previously answered questions. The answers take the form of step-by-step instructions or video guides. The home page is bright and newsy – at Halloween, for example, it displays lots of advice about making costumes and carving pumpkins. Some articles are clearly meant for fun: 'How to attract good luck', 'How to blow your nose in public'.

Quora.com Members can pose any query – ranging from the practical ('How do I change a spark plug?') to the educational ('What's the best book to read if I want to learn about Japan') or the philosophical ('Do you believe in free will?') – and then read through the answers given by other users. You can post anonymously but most users don't – as well as their names, they can add a note about their credentials. This makes it easier to assess the credibility of the replies and the discussions can be thought-provoking and considered as a result.

I like reading about food.

And lots of people like writing about it! There are many online magazines and sites that celebrate the joy of food – try HuffPost Taste (from the Huffington Post) or saveur.com – or search for 'best food blogs' and see what you stumble across.

Computing and troubleshooting

I have a problem with my computer. Where can I find help online?

The 'Help' pages on the official website of your computer manufacturer or operating system (such as Apple, Toshiba or Windows) are your first port of call if you need to download a user guide or handbook for your device. You can also find independent companies online; these are firms that offer technical support – usually for a monthly fee. You can find advice for a printer in the same way.

It's only a small problem, though. I don't want to wade through a manual, and I definitely don't want to pay.

You can go down the 'online community' route. Go to a general question-and-answer site such as answers.com or quora.com, or try the computers category of fixed4free.com or fixingmycomputer.com, which features handy flowcharts to help you fix your machine one step a time. By typing a short summary of your specific query into the search box, you'll be more than likely to find posts by other individuals who have experienced the same problem – and hopefully been offered helpful advice to resolve the issue by other members.

The official website of your computer manufacturer or operating system is your first port of call if you have problems with your computer.

WEATHER AND TRAVEL

I'm going away. Where on the web can I get accurate weather information?

The weather is just another kind of news – and the web is the best place to get it, because it can react so quickly to changing situations. There are hundreds of websites and apps dedicated to the weather – locally, country-wide, globally.

You can use a weather app on your phone or tablet, which updates on a regular basis to let you know what the weather in your chosen location is going to be like – you can save your home town, or your holiday destination, say. On a PC or a Mac, you can visit the website of a meteorological bureau, or a specialist weather information website; type in the town/city name or postal code of the place you are interested in and save this as a default and you'll then be given weather forecasts tailored to your needs every time you visit that website. All the big news organisations have weather information on their home page, too, of course.

How do I get a weather app on my tablet or phone?

A weather app is often installed as standard on a tablet or smartphone. So you may find that you already have, say, weather.com or AccuWeather. If not, you can download one manually by searching in your app store.

How do I get local weather on the app?

Weather apps usually operate with location-detection software – this means that when you open the app, it will automatically detect your location and provide you with instant information about the weather conditions, wherever you are. You'll also be able to find an in-depth forecast for that location on an hour-by-hour basis, as well as longer-range forecasts.

What if I am interested in the weather in some place other than where I am?

On any weather app there will be a facility to search for weather in other places. If you regularly need to know the weather in those other locations, you can save them to a list of your favourite places and always access that information swiftly. This can be useful if you often have to travel back and forth between towns that are hundreds of kilometres apart or if you want to keep tabs on the weather, say, where your relatives live.

Speaking of travel, what kind of traffic news can I find online?

For road traffic news, visit the website of a general news provider. National highways agencies are another good place to find regularly updated information and breaking traffic news incidents. There are a number of available apps – including Snarl Traffic and Waze Social GPS Maps & Traffic – that can be set up to deliver live traffic information to your tablet or smartphone while you are on the move (though – of course! – if you are driving then you should stop before you consult your phone, or else let a passenger do it).

What about rail or flight information?

Many rail companies and transport networks offer a similar service – timetables, live departures, alerts of delays and cancellations. These too are available on your computer or via apps for your tablet or smartphone – search for the name of the company that serves your local area.

For flight information, go to the official website of an airport or the airline itself. Often you will find that all you need to do is type in the flight number to find out all the information related to that flight.

And what about getting driving directions or route-maps online?

There are online route planners such as MapQuest and NRMA Trip Planner, where you provide your starting point and destination (either a town or city name, a street address or postal code), and the site generates a set of door-to-door driving directions, along with a printable map of the route. It may well also offer additional information such as a summary of the total distance the journey will cover and an estimate of how long the drive will take. You have the option to customise the route, too. This is handy if you want to visit a particular spot along the way, or if you'd rather avoid a certain road.

It would be handy to have that kind of thing on my mobile.

You can, of course. Smartphone and tablet device apps, including MapQuest, Google Maps and Apple Maps, offer programmable satellite navigation facilities, which can detect your starting location and guide you in realtime to your specified destination. However, some route planners require you to be connected to the internet, and as you'll be on the move, a secure and constant connection cannot always be guaranteed. And bear in mind that using a phone as a satnav when you are abroad can be very costly.

This kind of app quickly drains battery life – do bring an in-car charger so you don't get caught out.

Can't I download my route so I can look at it when I'm not connected?

If you are using a smartphone, you can download a map from Google Maps to your device by tapping on the start and end points of your route or entering the city or town name. The map remains available on your phone, and you can zoom in and out, even if you lose your internet connection.

I have tried this, but it doesn't work that well.

It's true that there are disadvantages to using your smartphone this way. If you go offline, the map that you have downloaded will have been saved at a fairly low resolution and the time estimates you are given for the trip duration will not update as you travel. And you can't change your initial route without being online. What is more, this kind of app quickly drains battery life – do bring an in-car charger so you don't get caught out.

Google Earth

The web has transformed map technology – and you can now pay a virtual visit to anywhere in the world. Google Earth is available as a computer program that you download onto your desktop computer or laptop, and also in app form for smartphone and tablet users. It includes the same searchable maps that are available on the Google Maps website, but offers many more features on top. With a swipe of your finger or a click of your mouse, you can transport yourself virtually to anywhere in the world, using satellite images and 3D maps. Just type in a post code, address or city name in the search box in the left-hand panel and click **Search**.

Booking your journey

Everyone I know books flights online these days. How do I get the best deals?

Many sites exist to help you to check flight prices and availability. The price of a ticket varies enormously on a day-to-day basis, and it's worth checking on a price-comparison website, such as Skyscanner, Expedia, Kayak or Webjet, before booking. Certain travel websites, including Expedia, allow you to subscribe to an email alert service, which informs users when specific (and usually short-lived) deals are available. It's also wise to check the prices offered on the airline's own website, as sometimes they offer a better deal than a third-party broker.

I've found a great price. How do I make the booking?

First of all, double-check that the fare you've seen really does exist. An advertisement offering too-good-to-miss airfares to your dream destination may have caught your eye, but when you try and book it online or ring the call-centre number, the price you are quoted might be far higher. Most discounts are available for a limited number of seats and sell out fast.

Can I make my booking over the phone as well as online, then?

Some flight-search websites require you to call them to complete the booking, while certain airlines and flight brokers allow you to complete the entire booking process online. When booking online, do check that the website is secure (see page 54), and enter your full name, address, credit or debit card information, email address and passenger information (usually the full name, date of birth, gender and passport number for each person travelling in your party). Be sure to make a note of the reference number that appears on your screen when your booking is confirmed. Confirmation of your booking and your e-ticket will be sent to you by email.

Double-check the fare you've seen really does exist. When you try and book online, the price you are quoted might be far higher.

Top tips for booking online

It has never been easier to make your own travel arrangements – and here are some ways to ensure that the run-up to your trip is stress-free.

1. Always check the small print when booking a flight – make sure you understand the terms and conditions. You need to know such things as whether your fare includes a meal, whether it costs extra to put luggage in the hold, whether the cost of the flight is refundable.

2. Never click twice when making your reservation, as there is a chance that your payment card could be debited twice.

3. Book only with a reputable firm. You may find it helpful to read reviews written by other travellers about their personal experiences with an airline or ticketing company before you book. TripAdvisor's Air Travel forums are a good place to browse discussions about booking experiences, customer service satisfaction and the flights themselves.

4. Carefully double-check your itinerary once you receive the email acknowledgement. If the spelling of any names or other details does not exactly match how they appear in your passport, then you need to contact the company who issued the tickets immediately to get them amended. Some airlines are more lenient than others, but it is very likely that you would not be allowed to board your flight with a ticket on which your initials are given incorrectly, for example.

What exactly is an e-ticket and what do I need to do with it?

Once you've paid for your trip, you'll receive a copy of the itinerary and a confirmation number by email. This is your e-ticket and is required when checking in with the airline. You'll need to print this out and take it with you when you arrive at the airport to check in – or if your airline offers an online check-in service, you'll need to have your e-ticket reference number handy when you check yourself in.

How do I check in online? And is it a good idea to do this?

Some airlines enable you to check in online 24 hours before your flight is due to depart, saving you time and the stress of queuing up at a check-in desk at the airport. You'll probably be sent an email letting you know that the online check-in has opened – with a link for you to follow in order to whizz through the process. Otherwise, you'll need to visit the official website of the airline you're flying with and enter your flight details and your e-ticket reference number. You may be offered the option of pre-selecting your seats or asked if you need to add any extra luggage, often for an additional fee. Some airlines also give you the chance to print your own boarding pass, which saves you more time – if you do so, check that the barcode prints properly as this will need to be scanned at the airport.

What information is available for, say, train travel?

Whatever mode of transport you have in mind, in whatever country, you'll find websites and apps online that allow you to research the times of services, download maps and plan the logistics of practically any trip you could ever wish to make. With a few clicks you can get your hands on travel information that would have been completely beyond your reach a few years ago: the times of shuttle trains to and from Moscow Airport, the price of buses between Sydney and Melbourne, the frequency of the car ferry from the Scottish mainland to the island of Islay... This type of specific information is online and available as a matter of course. Visit the website of the transport service operator (bus company, rail operator, ferry line, etc) for information; you may well find that there is also up-to-the-minute news on delays and cancellations. And of course you will be able to check ticket prices and fare options, and (usually) book your travel tickets at the site.

Is it worth booking train tickets online?

Generally speaking, the further ahead you book your train tickets, the cheaper they are. Train tickets can often be booked up to 12 weeks ahead. Advance tickets are usually available on longer-distance journeys, but have limited availability – so the earlier you book them, the better. The same applies to ferry crossings – try to make your travel arrangements as far in advance as possible to obtain the best fares.

Will I need to print my own tickets?

It largely depends on where you are and what train service you are going to be travelling on. Some rail companies allow you to order online and pay with a credit or debit card. Then you take the card you paid with to the railway station, enter it into a ticket machine and the machine prints your tickets. Other companies may require you to print your own tickets. Some companies send the tickets to your home address in the post.

How do I get up-to-the-minute service updates when I'm out and about?

Many public transport service providers offer apps that allow you to view the live status of their services from your smartphone or tablet – so you no longer need to wait for long at a bus stop (or if you do, at least you know how long you are going to have to wait).

Hotels and mini-breaks

Where's the best place to look for a good hotel deal?

There are hundreds of specialist travel and hotel sites that can help you find any kind of hotel – from a cheap bed for the night at the airport to a luxury suite at a 5-star hotel. And the internet makes last-minute planning very easy. Say you arrive in an unfamiliar town in the evening: you can easily find a hotel room for that same night – either through a website or using one of the many tablet or smartphone apps. Hotwire Hotels, Hotels.com, Wotif.com.au and lastminute.com.au can be accessed on both formats.

How can I tell if a hotel is worth staying at?

Before you book, check what previous visitors to the hotel or resort had to say about their stay. The power of the internet means it is easier than ever to share your experiences, both good and bad, and it's well worth looking at some independent holiday reviews before you believe every word the glossy brochure (or the website) tells you – up to 90 per cent of people check a review site before making an online booking. TripAdvisor is a good place to start: type in the hotel or resort name in the search box, and then browse through a collection of reviews written by people who have stayed there.

Where should I look for private holiday rentals?

It's never been easier for travellers to track down a holiday rental. Airbnb's database includes properties for short-term rentals in 34,000 cities around the world. Type your desired destination and check-in/check-out dates in the search box, and you'll be shown a list of properties (from shared or private rooms to entire houses, flats or villas) that match your requirements and budget. HomeAway and Wimdu are other popular sites.

How can I find useful information about the town I am in?

If you're out and about in unfamiliar surroundings, and have your smartphone or tablet device to hand, you'll soon be able to get your bearings and find out what services and amenities are nearby. Using GPS location pinpointing, apps such as AroundMe will show you the hospitals, police stations and petrol stations that are closest to where you are. You'll probably find yourself turning to the app for less-than-emergency situations too, like finding your nearest coffee shop, car or movie theatre.

Learning a language

I need to learn a few phrases in the local language. Can the web help?

A wide range of phrase-books and interactive tutorials can be found online. They exist for pretty much every language from Albanian to Zulu. A variety of foreign language apps are also available for you to download if you have a tablet or a smartphone. For a holiday, it may be enough to learn some key phrases parrot-fashion ('A coffee, please', 'A table for two'.)

Actually, I want to learn a bit more than just the basics…

In that case, various online language courses and resources are available. You can shop around to find an approach and style of learning that suits you. These might include formal tutorials, e-books and self-study materials. Many online courses offer a short introductory lesson on a trial basis, so you'll be able to tell if it's something that would work for you.

Long-established language-learning software companies, such as Rosetta Stone and Berlitz, allow you to register and study online – and they have apps for tablet and mobile phone users. Complete self-study language courses can be purchased online and downloaded to your PC or Mac from software companies such as Linguaphone.

Many online courses offer a short introductory lesson on a trial basis, so you'll be able to tell if it's something that would work for you.

How can I improve my fluency?

Once you've mastered the basics, a great way to accustom your ear to the language you are learning is to tune into a foreign radio station online. There are also social networking sites – busuu.com and livemocha.com – that are designed specifically for foreign-language practice. On these sites, you interact with native speakers of the language you are interested in. And, of course, you can access foreign websites to read the news, follow French-speaking people on Twitter and so on.

I want to read a French newspaper, but have only been able to find English translations online.

If you know the name of the news organisation – Le Monde, for example – type it into your search engine and the site should be high in the list of results generated. Or type, say, Google France into your search engine – this should bring up the French version of Google, which will list French sites, but you will have to type in keywords in French, of course.

What if I am abroad and stuck for a word? How can I quickly find out what something means?

There are plenty of online foreign dictionaries that you can search for free. There are also lots of dictionary apps that you can download to your tablet or mobile device. These include digital versions of popular print titles from specialist publishers such as Collins and Berlitz. Online translators, such as Google Translate, are available if you want to translate words and longer passages of text.

Do translation websites work?

They work up to a point. But be aware that computer-generated translations are pretty basic. They rarely produce an entirely natural and grammatical sentence in the target language, and they have trouble dealing with ordinary words that have numerous meanings and senses, such as 'check' or 'light'. They might help you figure out the species of fish on a menu, but they are no good for translating, say, a police statement if you are unlucky enough to have your purse stolen.

7

CONSUMING MEDIA ONLINE

Starting points

- **There's a world of digital media** that you can access via the internet: films, television, music, audiobooks and more.
- **You can watch TV programs** you have missed and old movies for free, or pay to view new movies and TV series.
- **It's easy to play music** on your computer or mobile devices – you can build your own collection, or sign up to a music site and choose from thousands of tracks.
- **You can use the internet to store large files online,** to make them available across all your devices and to avoid using up space on your computer.

KEY ACTIONS

- Discover how to watch television online.
- Make the most of YouTube.
- Learn about the legalities, and how to avoid piracy.
- Build and organise a digital music collection.
- Listen to the radio and talking books.
- Find out about the cloud and use it for online storage.

TELEVISION AND FILM

Can I watch TV on my computer?

Yes, and it's not that different from watching it on a television set. Your television, if it is fairly new, is a kind of computer with a big screen while your computer or tablet can be used as a portable TV. The same digital technology underlies all these devices. So you no longer need a TV set in order to watch shows so long as you have a connection to the internet and an up-to-date browser. You will also need a fast broadband connection with a high download limit (see page 25) so you can copy programs or films onto your computer.

Watching TV or films online (or listening to radio programs or music tracks), without downloading any files, is called 'streaming'. You can subscribe to websites where you can stream classic TV series or movies as well as up-to-date ones. You can also access TV channels where you can watch recent TV programs you may have missed – 'catch-up TV', as it is known.

Does catch-up TV cost anything if I do it on my computer?

No, it is free, just as it is on a TV set. If you missed a program and didn't record it, you can usually find it on catch-up and stream it on your tablet or computer. Programs are usually available for a few weeks after being aired on TV.

How exactly do I watch catch-up?

Tablets are useful for watching TV online as they are portable and have a good-sized screen; they are designed for this kind of use (see also page 17). But the process is much the same on a desktop computer or laptop, and works perfectly well on those devices. Here are three ways to watch catch-up:

1. TV channels make catch-up available via their website (if you use a computer) or apps for tablets and smartphones. On a computer, just go to your local TV channel's website and look for the catch-up listings. On a tablet or smartphone, download the TV channel's catch-up app from the app store, then open it to access the program listings. Once you're in the app or website, you'll see programs recommended by the channel, and you'll be able to search for a specific program if you know what you want to watch.

2. If you set up an account with YouTube, you can subscribe (for free) to the catch-up services of television channels in your country and watch episodes via the site (see page 226 for more about YouTube).

3. You can also view catch-up through your TV set if you have a digital TV that is able to connect to the internet (or through your games console if it supports an internet connection). On your TV, go to the screen with all the apps (sometimes called the home screen) and locate the catch-up TV apps. Then take your pick.

I have programs downloaded to my laptop, but I'd rather watch them on the TV. Can I do that?

Yes, a laptop screen feels a bit small for blockbuster movies, it's true. If you want to watch them on your TV, then you just need the right cable to connect from your TV to your laptop. There are several different types of connection that your computer could have, so take a photo of all the ports (where you could plug in a lead) that you have on your device and go into a computer accessories store and ask them which cable you need. Similarly, TVs have varying types of sockets (ports) so take a photo of this too and also make a note of the make and model.

You just need the right cable to connect from your TV to your laptop.

I've got the right cable. What now?

When you plug in the cable and switch on the laptop and TV, your TV may automatically switch to display the laptop screen. If not, you will need to refer to the instruction book that came with your TV to find out how to do this manually. If the picture looks blurry, then you may also need to change the screen settings on your laptop. Here is how:

- In Windows, right-click on your desktop and select **Screen resolution**. Alter the size to correct the image you see on the TV by trial and error. Depending on your version of Windows, you may instead see settings for **Laptop display only**, **TV display only**, or **Laptop and TV display** together. Selecting either of the latter two should work.

- On a MacBook, go to **System Preferences** then **Displays** and select the **Arrangement** tab. If you can't see that tab, click **Detect Displays**. Tick **Mirror Displays** and this will give the best picture for your TV set.

- Make sure you write down the previous settings first so you can revert back to them afterwards.

How about catch-up TV from other countries. How can I get that?

It's not usually possible to watch TV programs aired in other countries. This is because of licensing regulations. But you can occasionally find a foreign channel that does air in your country. If so, go to its website, find the catch-up menu and then try to watch an episode. A message will let you know if the show isn't available at your location.

I love settling down to watch a whole TV series on DVD. Can I find series on the web as well?

Yes, there are websites where you can stream or download TV programs and series (as well as movies). These include Quickflix and Foxtel, which require you to pay a monthly subscription. Alternatively, you can pay a small fee to watch individual programs or whole TV series in iTunes or YouTube.

A quick guide to YouTube

YouTube, owned by Google, is a fun website with an extensive collection of video clips available to watch online. You can browse and watch the clips for free, and – if you have a Google account – you can also rate them, leave comments or upload your own video.

1. Anyone can contribute a video to YouTube and many of the clips are posted by ordinary people – popstar Justin Bieber was discovered after he put home videos of himself on the site.

2. YouTube clips are often short (up to 15 minutes) and humorous – you can find pretty much anything from home videos featuring cats or laughing babies to political commentary or academic lectures. You'll also find TV clips, movie trailers and chart music videos there.

3. The site is easy to use. You type keywords into the search box, and a selection of videos appears below. You click on one to watch and when it finishes, you are offered more videos on related topics. You can then keep clicking and clicking from one video to another – a good way to discover things you like but wouldn't necessarily search for.

4. YouTube also acts as a conduit for various media companies, allowing you to watch catch-up TV or pay to download or stream TV shows and movies. You'll need to sign up for a Google account if you want to access paid-for programs (you will have this already if you already use a Google service, such as Gmail or Google+). Account holders can also 'subscribe' to catch-up TV channels – this just means they are listed on your YouTube home page, so you can access them with one click.

5. Be aware that while explicit content is not allowed on YouTube, there can be items unsuitable for children. To filter out such content, scroll to the bottom of the YouTube page and click **Safety** to turn filtering on.

So I can watch movies online, too?

You certainly can. Quickflix and Presto allow you to watch films online (streaming) and this works out cheaper than buying DVDs. Presto and Quickflix are subscription sites, where you pay a monthly fee and get access to their catalogue of films, but Quickflix also offers a pay-per-view service, so you pay for each film you would like to watch, one at a time.

Which should I choose – pay-per-view or a monthly subscription?

It depends on how many films you watch. If you are likely to watch more than one film per month, a subscription site is usually a good deal. If you just want to watch the occasional film, you're probably better off with pay-per-view. Movie sites don't have every film ever made, but they do have a good selection of recent films and older ones.

What about if I want to keep the film, so I can watch it again?

Then it is better to go to sites where you can buy and download films instead of streaming them – iTunes is one such site. In this case you pay for the copy of the film and can then watch it as many times as you like. It will be a little more expensive than pay-per-view films and is really like buying a copy of the DVD but without receiving the physical disk – you keep a file on your device instead.

I use one of these sites, but it doesn't have all the films I want to see.

Licensing restrictions can mean that some popular or current films are not available for streaming. They may be available on DVD. There are websites that offer DVD rental, where you sign up and pay online for the films you want to watch and receive the DVDs through the post. These sites generally have a larger catalogue; the downside is that you cannot watch them instantly: you have to wait for them to be posted to you and you have to return them to get the next film you want. Bigpond Movies is one such website. Type 'DVD rental website' into a search engine to find others.

Avoid piracy on the internet

It's easy to download films, music, books and so on from the internet, but it's important to stay within the law. Check that the sites you use are legal – and steer clear of the suspicious ones.

There are many legal websites offering films, music, books and other media for free or for a fee. Downloading official copies of such files means the artists or writers get paid for their work (which is how they make their living). And it means that the entertainment industry can carry on producing good-quality TV, films, music and books. There are, however, some dishonest websites that offer pirated copies of the same files. You should not download from dubious sites for two reasons: first, it is illegal and you could be prosecuted if you do it; second, pirate copies may well contain computer viruses that can attack your machine or aim to steal personal or financial information. Here is how to distinguish between the good download sites and the bad ones.

- **Buy from known and trusted websites.** A company that is a household name is highly unlikely to be engaging in piracy. Buying direct – books from the publishing company, for example – is also a good way to avoid piracy.

- **Bona fide websites** will display a legal statement saying that they have obtained the copyright permission from the owners. If there is no such statement, that could mean that the site is a counterfeit operation. If you're not able to find this text, contact the website to ask if they have permission to offer downloads of the files. (If there is no contact information, don't use the site.)

- **If a site offers the latest films** or music for download before they've made it to the shops, be very suspicious. Don't download from the site.

- **The fact that a site charges** for downloads does not on its own mean that it is official. Sites offering illegal downloads sometimes charge fees, too.

- **Internet auction sites** can attract unscrupulous sellers. It's safer to stick to well-known online companies when looking to buy copyrighted material.

- **If you download something** and find that it is poor quality, then it is likely to be pirated. Sometimes the signs are laughably obvious: if you see silhouetted heads of people at the bottom of your screen, this indicates an illegal copy that has been surreptitiously (and illegally) filmed by someone sitting in a cinema seat.

- **At Pro-Music** (pro-music.org) you can find a list of sites that legally provide downloads of music and other media too. There is a list of sites to avoid at the Center for Democracy and Technology (cdt.org). Neither list is exhaustive and the CDT's list concentrates on American sites.

- **It's against the law** to share digital files of music, videos and so on with other people (in the same way you shouldn't copy, say, a DVD). So don't copy a CD track onto your computer and then pass the file on to a friend.

I don't really want to spend money on watching movies. Is there anywhere that I can watch films for free?

There is if you like the classics. Try the site Viewster, which is available in more than 100 countries and offers a catalogue of old films and TV shows for free. It relies on income from advertising, so you have to put up with lots of ad breaks. But using the site is simple: you just need to register to start viewing.

Is it better to download a TV show or film, or to stream it?

Many online TV shows and films are available only through streaming, so often you don't have the choice. But if there is an option to download then there are advantages to doing it that way. You can watch a downloaded program anywhere once you have taken the time to get it onto your device: you are not dependent on there being a constant internet connection. So downloads are really the only option for watching a film on a long train or plane journey, for example. And if you have a connection but it is not quite fast enough to stream TV without interruption, then you are better off with a download, because a download will run without stopping to 'buffer' the next chunk of video, and the quality of the moving image is likely to be better.

I have heard about people being prosecuted for downloading things from the internet. Should I worry?

You don't need to worry so long as you are downloading files from a legal website. There are some bogus sites out there that offer pirated copies of the latest films and TV series, but if you stick to the official websites such as the ones mentioned above then it's all very much above board. Go to page 228 for more information on legal (and illegal) downloading.

You can watch a downloaded program anywhere once you have taken the time to get it onto your device.

MANAGE YOUR MUSIC ONLINE

Where can I find music online?

There are many different ways. You can:

- Buy and download tracks and albums from online sellers such as Amazon and iTunes.
- Subscribe to online music-streaming sites such as Spotify to listen to an enormous catalogue of recorded music.
- Listen to music clips and orchestral performances on YouTube, for free. Or go to Spotify to listen to free music from new bands.
- Play online radio from around the world (see page 242).

How do I actually play music on my device, though?

You'll need music-player software on your machine. This program is like a kind of digital jukebox, and it comes as standard on new computers, tablets and phones. You may also want to invest in speakers for your computer (if the built-in ones are not large enough or sophisticated enough to play music to a high standard). If you are storing music on your phone and you want to play it sometimes in a room at home, you might want to buy a docking station. This is a set of speakers and an amplifier in one compact unit, and your phone or MP3 or MP4 player (such as an iPod) plugs neatly into it (though you may need to remove your phone's cover first, if you have one). You can also buy a small, separate speaker that plugs into your phone or iPod and is very portable and good for travelling (although the sound is mono, not stereo).

What music player do I need?

Most PCs come pre-loaded with Windows Media Player. Macs have the iTunes music player by default, and this is a popular player available for free for Windows too – go to apple.com to download it. iTunes is also used by iPods and iPads, which means that you can keep your music in iTunes and easily share it (synchronise) between all Apple-made devices. Similarly, you can synchronise your choice of music between your PC and MP3 or MP4 player using Windows Media Player.

Okay, so how do I buy music?

It's easy to buy digital music. If you have iTunes, simply open the application and then click on the **iTunes Store** button in the right-hand corner. This will take you to the online store; select **Music** from the menu bar at the top of the window, and browse or enter specific keywords (such as the name of a track or artist) in the search bar and press **Enter/Return.** Click on any album that interests you, and you can then opt to buy individual tracks or the whole album.

You will need an Apple id (identity) to use the iTunes store: open iTunes, click **iTunes Store**, then **Create Account**. You can pay by various methods including credit and debit cards and vouchers bought online or from a shop. When you have finished in the store, click the **Library** button in the right-hand corner.

Once downloaded to your device, the file or files (if you're downloading a whole album) can be played through your music player, which will also function as the 'library' of your music collection.

How else can I get digital music?

You can go to an online music store such as Google Play or Amazon. (If you have a new version of Windows Media Player, click on the **Switch to Library** button at the top-right corner of the player, then the arrow to the right of **Online Stores** and then **Browse all online stores** to find them.) Search for the music that you want and then click to buy. Once you have purchased the music, you can listen to it online or download it in the form of a digital file – usually at the click of a button. You will be asked where you wish to save the file. Save it somewhere logical like the My Music folder on your computer (if using Windows), or the Automatically Add to iTunes folder (if you are on a Mac), so it can be easily located later.

Some websites will ask you to install their special file downloader. If you're likely to visit the same site for music downloads, it's worth doing this since it'll speed up the process, but you don't usually have to.

Does it work the same way on a smartphone?

If you want to buy music on a tablet or smartphone, the easiest way is through an online store such as iTunes or the Google Play Store. A store app will be pre-loaded on your phone or tablet. Tap to open it, and then find the music you want either by searching for it or by browsing the suggestions. (See page 236 for advice on transferring music from a computer to a mobile device.)

Using a music player

I have Windows Media Player. How do I use it to play my downloaded files?

Open Windows Media Player and look on the main screen for the music file you have downloaded – it should be automatically listed there. Highlight the track you wish to play by clicking on it, then you can either press the play ▶ button at the bottom (alternatively, right-click and select **Play**) or double-click on the song.

If the file is not listed on the main screen, click on **Organize** then **Manage Libraries** then **Music**. In the window that pops up you'll see a list of music folders on your computer, such as the My Music folder. If you save music elsewhere, you can click the **Add** button to navigate to the folder where you save music and add it to this list. Once a folder is on this list, Windows Media Player will automatically show files from that folder. So, when you download a file from a music store, if you place it in one of the folders on this list – say, My Music – then it'll automatically be added to Windows Media Player and be available to play.

What about iTunes?

If you buy a music file from a source other than the iTunes store, then it may also be automatically added to your iTunes library and be on the main screen, ready for you to play. If so, highlight the track by clicking on it once, then press the play button ▶ at the top left of the screen (alternatively, double-click the track, or right-click and select **Play**).

If the file hasn't been added automatically, you'll need to locate it. Click **File** then **Add file** to library and in the pop-up window navigate to the place you have saved the file on your computer. Next, click **Open** and the file will appear in your library, ready to play.

How do I get iTunes to add all the music I download to my library?

First, make sure you have the latest version of iTunes (click on **Help** and **Check for updates** to get new updates). New versions of iTunes are programmed to check a folder called Automatically Add to iTunes and add any music in this folder to your library. So, when you download a file you have purchased, be sure to store it in this folder on your computer (you'll find it in the iTunes folder on your computer, inside the iTunes Media folder). If you do that, iTunes will automatically add the files to your library every time.

I like to organise my vinyl albums and CDs by type. Can I do that with my digital music collection?

Tracks are automatically grouped by album, and you'll notice that the media players even download the album cover for each album, to make it easier to distinguish each one by eye. The player groups tracks by artist, genre and album title, to name but a few categories, so at any time you can choose to sort your library using one of these headings.

How can I sort my library?

Decide which category you want to group your tracks by, and click on the appropriate tab. That's it. So there's really little organisation to be done by hand (which is helpful if you have an extensive music collection), unless you wish to create playlists.

What's a playlist?

You'll see this term crop up a lot in relation to digital music. It is simply a set of tracks that you have chosen to group together. For example, you could create a playlist of love songs, or background music for a party, or your all-time favourite songs or even music to do the housework to.

I want to create a playlist. How do I do it?

The process is slightly different depending on your music player.

- In Windows Media Player, open your main music library by clicking on **Music** in the left-hand column. Locate the tracks you wish to add to your playlist, then drag and drop them into the right-hand column, underneath the heading **Unsaved list**. When you have all the songs you want, click on **Save list** and you'll be given the option to name your list – choose something memorable.

- In iTunes on a Mac, go to **File** then **New** then **Playlist** and type the name that you want to give it. To add songs to your playlist, simply drag and drop them to the playlist at the right of the iTunes window. Click **Done** when you've finished.

- In iTunes for Windows, click on **Music** in the left-hand column to bring up your whole library. Select the first track you wish to add to your playlist, right-click on it and choose **New Playlist from Selection**. A new playlist will be created under the **Playlists** list at the left-hand side, and the name of it will be highlighted so you can type over it with your desired name. Once you've done this, return to your main music library and look for other songs to add to your playlist. Drag and drop each one onto the name of your playlist to add it.

Once you have created the playlist, it will appear in the left-hand column, under the menu option **Playlists**. Simply click on it and then press the play icon to listen.

How do I transfer songs and playlists from iTunes onto my iPod or iPhone?

It's simple. Make sure that iTunes is open on your computer then, using the charger lead, plug the iPod or iPhone into a USB port (look for the symbol). iTunes should recognise your device and the option **iPod** or **iPhone** should appear. Click on this and then click **Sync**. This will update your device with all the music from your iTunes library.

You can choose to automatically sync your device with your iTunes library by ticking or unticking the box that says **Automatically sync when this iPhone is connected**. All you'll need to do is connect your phone and it'll start to sync as soon as iTunes recognises the phone. You'll also be asked if you want to add any photos, apps and so on from your phone to iTunes on your computer, so you have a back-up of them.

When you copy your music onto your phone or iPod, it remains on your computer, too. Your computer is the place to update and manage your library before 'syncing' your devices with your main iTunes library.

So are iTunes and Windows Media Player just for music?

No, they're multipurpose. You can also watch videos using these players. That includes home movies stored on your device as well as films downloaded from the internet.

Streaming services

Is there anywhere I can listen to music free online, in the same way that I can get some newspapers for nothing?

Yes – there are several sites where you can stream music free on your device without downloading it. The trade-off is that you have to put up with advertisements between the tracks. Among the sites that offer free music are Spotify, Deezer and Pandora, depending on the country you are in.

Similarly, some artists – both established and up-and-coming – upload their music videos to YouTube, where you can watch them for free – they do this to publicise their work. YouTube groups together music from various artists and in various genres as 'channels' that you, as a window-shopper, can subscribe to for free so long as you have a Google account.

How do I subscribe to a YouTube music channel?

Open YouTube in your browser and look for the **Browse Channels** option in the column at the left. Click on this, and a list of channels will come up. You can look at the videos here. When you see a channel you are interested in, simply click on **Subscribe** – and that's it. Then the channels you've subscribed to will be listed in the left-hand column (so long as you are logged in). Whenever you visit the site you can click on them to browse and watch their videos.

YouTube groups together music from various artists and in various genres as 'channels' that you, as a window-shopper, can subscribe to for free.

Classical music

The internet can be a virtual concert hall where you go to enjoy anything from Gregorian plainsong to a Brahms symphony. Since classical pieces tend to be longer than popular songs, you will need a good broadband connection to stream entire works. But a world of music – both familiar and as yet undiscovered – awaits you.

Listening to classical music

These are some of the best methods and sites for listening to classical music online, without it costing you anything.

1. Listen to classical radio channels – go to shoutcast.com and look through the classical category to find them (you can search on subcategories such as 'baroque' if you like), or try classicalwebcast.com.

2. Subscribe to YouTube's classical music channel for free (see page 226 for more about the sites's subscription service).

3. Find free classical music at MusOpen (musopen.com): you can listen online, download tracks and even print out sheet music here.

4. Go to classicalconnect.com. It, too, has a lot of free online music. It also invites independent musicians and orchestras to upload their content, so you can listen to music from different performers, compare performers or even upload your own performance! The site has a search box so if you're searching for a specific piece you can type this in. Or you can browse the listings by instrument, performer or composer.

5. Buy tracks at the specialist site classical.com, which is both an online store and a streaming service offering more than 750,000 classical pieces. You can buy tracks for download or subscribe to listen to the whole catalogue.

Watching performances

You can also find live performances on the internet, which might otherwise be difficult for you to get to.

- **You can watch free live performances** on medici.tv, or subscribe to access their back catalogue of performances online.

- **Well-known orchestras,** such as the Berlin Philharmonic (digitalconcerthall.com) and Moscow Symphony Orchestra (moscowsymphony.ru), have their own websites where you can watch live performances or previous performances online, some of which are free.

- **Some opera houses,** such as New York's Metropolitan Opera, have a subscription service (which you watch via a free app) as well as some free video clips online (metoperafamily.org). Try searching the official website of an opera or ballet company or orchestra to check for free performances.

For the price of one CD a month, you can subscribe and have access to a huge catalogue of music.

What about Spotify and the like – what do they offer?

These are music-streaming services that allow you to listen to a wide variety of music online for free, with advertisements interspersed. To listen on your computer, you download customised music-player software for each site, and there is an app for smartphones and tablets.

The great thing about these sites is the sheer quantity and variety of music that is there for you to enjoy. You have to endure the ads – but that is no worse that listening to a commercial radio station; only on this station, you are in charge of the playlist.

So if I can listen to music for free online, why would I subscribe to a paid-for service?

Well, there are the ads – and the fact that you may have less flexibility in terms of using other devices. In addition, you may be able to listen only for as long as you are signed up and when you are connected to the net (and, of course, you often lose connection when you are on the move). Also the free services may have restrictions on how long you can listen to music in any one day.

But the music sounds as good, whether I pay a subscription or not?

Actually, no. The quality of the music can be much better when you pay the monthly subscription. And yet for the price of one CD a month, you can subscribe and have access to a huge catalogue of music, all of it there in your music library, and without any annoying advertisements.

So how do I choose between the different music services available?

It comes down to personal preference. Spotify has access to new releases, sometimes days before they are available for general sale, so it's a great resource for anyone who likes to keep up to date with the latest music. Deezer allows you to listen on the site – you don't need to download any additional software. You can link Spotify and Deezer with your Facebook account and find out what your friends are listening to, which can give you insights into new music. Since these sites and other music-streaming services allow you to listen for free, it's a good idea to try out a couple before signing up for a paid subscription.

I listen on a mobile device, so I am not always connected to the internet.

Music-streaming sites have an offline mode, so that you can download a certain number of tracks and listen to them when you are offline (on an aeroplane, say). You have to set this up beforehand, though. Go to the site (when you are connected to the internet), click on the playlist you want to download, and follow the instructions to select the offline mode.

If I can subscribe to a service like this, why would I ever pay to download an album again?

This depends on how long you plan to subscribe to a music-streaming service. It's fantastic if you want to listen to new music, and gives you access to a huge catalogue of tracks, but only for as long as you keep subscribing. If there's an album you know you want to keep forever, then it is probably worth buying it as a download or a CD.

OTHER ONLINE LISTENING

What about listening to radio on the net? Can I listen to stations from other countries?

One of the many fantastic things about the internet is that you can stream radio from around the world as well as your own country. Sites such as live-radio.net and tunein.com allow you to do this: simply go to the site, look at their vast list of global radio, and click on the station you are interested in. You will hear whatever is being broadcast at that moment (make sure the volume is turned up on your computer or laptop, and it isn't on mute). With radio, there aren't the restrictions that surround the streaming of movies and TV.

Fantastic. Can I listen to the radio on my tablet or phone?

Yes, the process is similar to viewing the TV, but with faster loading times as images aren't required. You can listen by going to the website of your favourite radio station (if on a computer or laptop) or by downloading the app provided (usually free) by the radio station you want to listen to (on a tablet or smartphone). A smartphone is a good, portable radio player in this case, using a radio station's app and your internet connection, but remember this kind of data consumption is high, so unless you have a high-download package from your mobile-phone provider, you should use your home WiFi. Most radio-station websites provide catch-up radio programs and other podcasts in addition to the live, realtime broadcast.

I keep hearing the word 'podcast' but I'm not sure what it is.

That's not surprising because 'podcast' is a term that seems to be used very loosely. If you miss a radio broadcast, it should be available via catch-up online, either through the radio station's website or its app. You may find that the radio station calls the catch-up programs podcasts – but strictly speaking, podcasts are programs specifically recorded for the internet, not just catch-up radio programs.

Either way, there is no difference in the way that you obtain them and listen to them: you can stream them, or download them to listen to later on your computer or even your iPod.

How do I find good podcasts?

For those with an Apple device or iTunes, there is an app called Podcasts that makes the process of choosing podcasts very easy. There are other free apps, including BeyondPod Podcast Manager, PodKicker and OneCast, which allow you to find and listen to podcasts whether on your phone or on your computer via your web browser. Install the software from the Google Play website or from the app store on your phone. You can browse all of these apps to find interesting and informative recordings to listen to on all kinds of topics, from comedy to academic lectures.

Talking books

I love listening to talking books on CD. Can I download them directly from the web as well?

Yes, they are often called audiobooks, and the reading may be done by a famous actor (they are usually an abridged version of the print book). This kind of book is a great way to enjoy stories while you're doing other tasks – it's literature in radio form. And of course audiobooks are a wonderful resource for anyone with a visual impairment.

Where do I find them?

You can buy digital audiobooks from the iTunes store, which has a huge selection. The website audible.com, which is owned by Amazon, also has audiobooks for downloading. You can buy them one at a time but the books are much cheaper if you subscribe and pay a monthly or annual fee. Another subscription site is audiobooks.com, which lets you listen online or download the books to your device. And, of course, you can buy audiobooks on CD from online booksellers.

How do I download an audiobook?

You just need to have a media player, such as iTunes, Windows Media Player or similar installed on your device. You don't need to do anything – once you buy the book, it will automatically start to download. You can then listen to it on the device you have downloaded it to, or transfer it to an MP3 or MP4 player such as an iPod. (See page 233 for more on using a media player.)

Where to find free audiobooks

There are plenty of sources for free audiobooks online. You can either listen to them on the site, or download them to your device. You can also borrow digital audiobooks from your local library.

- **The Internet Archive** Created with the goal of making a permanent record of free web content, archive.org has more than 9000 audiobooks including some volumes of poetry.

- **Project Gutenburg** The long-established site gutenburg.org has a large selection of free talking books. Some are read by people, others by computers. The computer-read books aren't for everyone, as there is no intonation and some words aren't pronounced correctly.

- **Open Culture** This site at openculture.com gathers together free cultural and educational audiobooks from all over the internet and provides links to download them from sites such as iTunes and audible.com.

- **Learn Out Loud** You can find free, educational audiobook titles on a variety of subject areas including politics, philosophy and languages at learnoutloud.com.

- **Storynory** There is a collection of free children's stories available as audiobooks at storynory.com. Books are classified by school year group.

- **Librivox** A catalogue of free talking books that are in the public domain (out of copyright) in the USA can be found at librivox.org.

STORING YOUR FILES ONLINE

I have a huge collection of movies and music. Can I store it on the internet?

Certainly. There is a space on the internet where you can archive your files so that they don't fill up your computer's memory, and so that you don't have to back up files on CDs or other devices. It is called 'the cloud'.

I've heard of the cloud, but I'm not sure what it is.

Like the internet itself, the cloud is not a single entity but a collection of many sites and servers located in different parts of the physical world and cyberspace. Think of it as a huge virtual attic where you can box up your digital files till you need them. You can put anything there: photos, films, music, manuscripts… It's a great way to keep your computer or other device from getting too cluttered and full. And also, if you use the cloud to 'host' your files, as it is called, you can access them from anywhere and on any device – so long as you have an internet connection. You could start watching a film at home on your laptop, then finish watching it in a café on your smartphone.

What do you mean by 'hosting'?

This just means storing your files online in the cloud. There are many companies online that offer free or paid-for cloud-hosting services. It is exactly like having your own lock-up in a commercial warehouse. Among the companies that offer hosting are DropBox, Google Drive, iCloud and OneDrive – see page 247 for more about these.

You could start watching a film at home on your laptop, then finish watching it in a café on your smartphone.

Is it secure to keep my files online?

Yes. So long as you use a reputable provider, all your data is kept private and is often encrypted (scrambled) as well so others can't read it. The cloud is hosted on many servers and all of them have security measures in place to prevent hackers getting in. It is as safe as a deposit box in a bank – but even banks get robbed, so it is not possible to say that any digital storage facility is impregnable. Think twice about storing very sensitive information.

Is there anything I should do to improve security?

For a start, don't use the same password for multiple sites across the web: have different ones for all your log-ins (your cloud storage, your webmail, your bank and so on). That way, if one password is compromised, the hacker won't be able to get into your other accounts. (See page 76 for more information on secure passwords.) It is actually fairly safe to write down all your different passwords and hide them away somewhere at home: no ordinary house-burglar is likely to be interested. But to be doubly sure: use some kind of reminder system that no outsider could ever break (login: name of hospital where I was born; password: given name of first teacher...).

How do I store files in the cloud?

First choose a cloud storage provider, then sign up via their website, which will give instructions on how to do this and how to use the particular storage facility. On your smartphone or tablet, you'll be able to download the corresponding app relating to the storage provider you choose. Then you can easily store and access your files on whatever device you use.

What types of file can I store?

You can store any type of file in the cloud: music files, photos, films, e-books, apps, word-processing files, spreadsheets. The chances are you're probably already storing data in the cloud: if you use a web-based email service then you are using one type of free cloud-hosting service because all your emails are stored online in the cloud. If you use Google Docs to create documents then you're using another type of cloud-hosting service, as all the documents are stored in the cloud. If you're a Facebook user then all your Facebook info is stored in the cloud. If you use an iPhone or iPad, you may already be using Apple's iCloud storage service to back up all your files and programs (including your email and calendar) automatically.

Get free storage in the cloud

There are many providers out there. All of these offer free cloud storage options, plus subscription options if you need more space.

- **DropBox** The site offers up to 2GB of storage space for free but there are ways to get more free storage space by referring friends – each referral earns you 500MB of space, up to a total of 18GB. You can also use DropBox to share files and folders with friends.

- **Google Drive** This service from Google has many features (including Google Docs and Gmail), and a generous 15GB of free storage space.

- **iCloud** Apple provides 5GB of free storage space, and you can purchase more space for an annual subscription rate if you wish. Music, films, e-books and so on that you buy from iTunes don't count towards your 5GB of free storage space.

- **OneDrive** This is Microsoft's cloud storage service, so if you use Windows 8 or Office 2013 then you'll find access to OneDrive is built in and it's easy to store your files there directly. OneDrive allows up to 7GB of free storage for new users.

- **Bitcasa Infinite Drive** Possibly one of the more secure cloud-hosting services because files are encrypted before they are uploaded to Bitcasa's servers. Bitcasa offers a generous 20GB of free storage. However, it doesn't allow users to share files with anyone else.

There are any number of cloud storage providers that charge a monthly fee, with many and varied features and prices. Conveniently, there are also websites that review multiple cloud storage providers all in one place, to save you trawling through all the different provider websites to compare prices and features.

Card Holder
Credit Card

8

BUYING AND SELLING

Starting points

- **The internet is a gigantic marketplace** where you can buy and sell almost anything, from electronics to vintage clothing or groceries.
- **Online banking** means you can use the net to manage your finances – at any time of the day or night.
- **You can save money** by finding discount vouchers and by using sites that give you money back whenever you buy something online.
- **It's even possible to earn** extra money online – through surveys, competitions and mystery shopping.

KEY ACTIONS

- Stay secure when you bank online.
- Find whatever you need on the web.
- Spot common scams – and avoid them.
- Use auction sites to sell items you no longer want.
- Be savvy with your money and get good deals online.

BANKING ONLINE

Why should I bank online rather than in person at a branch?

No more standing in line at the bank, for one thing! You'll have access to your finances 24 hours a day, and you can transfer money and pay bills in a matter of seconds, without leaving the house. Also, while your bank might charge you for some transactions over the phone or in a branch, the same few clicks of the mouse will be free if you do it for yourself, on your own computer. But banking online doesn't mean you're left without a branch to visit; it's just an extra option. You can still go to your nearest bank branch whenever you want to.

So how do I bank online?

Contact your bank to find out what online services they offer, and they'll give you instructions on how to sign up. Your bank will have a secure website that you visit when you want to access your account; it may also have an app you can download to your smartphone, so that you can use that device too. If your bank does not offer online banking, you should consider switching to a bank that does. Many banks have incentives for switching to them, so shop around a little. Switching is easy since your new bank will take care of everything for you.

Once I've set up an account, how do I pay bills and transfer money?

When you log into your bank account, you'll see a menu with different options. Look for an option that says **Make payment** or **Pay bills** and follow the instructions on screen. Make absolutely sure that you enter the account number and BSB (bank and branch) number of the recipient correctly as well as the amount of money that you are transferring – you usually get a second chance to check it before the payment goes through. You can also set up standing orders or direct debits (see page 252).

That doesn't sound hugely secure.

The process is very safe, actually, because of the security measures your bank puts in place. When you go to the internet banking page, or make a payment to a new person, your bank will ask you to go through some checks to make sure that the person accessing your account is indeed you. Each bank has its own way of doing this.

- Some provide you with a 'reader' when you open an account. This is a little gadget that looks like a calculator but has a slot into which you insert your bank card; you also have to enter a PIN (personal identification number, like the one you use at an ATM) and sometimes a number that appears on your bank's web page. The reader will generate a number that you then type into the bank's website to gain access to your account.

- Other banks supply you with a 'secure key'. This too looks like a very tiny calculator. You type in a PIN and the key generates a second number, which you then type in at the website.

- Or your bank may send a text to a registered mobile number consisting of a string of numbers that you must type in online. After this check, you may also be asked for certain characters from your password.

Can I set up a direct debit or standing order on my own computer?

Of course. If there's a regular bill to be paid, you can set this up via your online banking account by entering all the details using their online form. Following this, you'll go through the same security measures as with making an ad hoc bill payment, before the direct debit or standing order is confirmed. It's a good idea to set an end date for the standing order, or to review your direct debits and standing orders regularly, so as to avoid paying for any services you stop using.

Your bank will ask you to go through some checks to make sure that the person accessing your account is indeed you.

What other services do you get with online banking?

Pretty much anything you get from a branch, short of giving you cash. You can check your balance, view your statements or download them to your computer, transfer money from one account to another, email your bank, update your details and so on.

And it is definitely safe?

Absolutely, yes. Online banking is made safe by the measures that banks take, such as encrypting (scrambling) their websites, logging you out if there is no activity after a short time and locking your account if several incorrect log-in attempts are made. When you open your bank's website, you'll see a locked padlock symbol or sometimes a solid (rather than broken) key symbol at the bottom, and the web address will change from http to https to show it's a secure site.

Six ways to protect your money

It's important that you take steps to keep your bank account secure. Here are six must-dos for anyone who banks online.

1. Check that you have up-to-date antivirus software installed on your computer, and that your firewall is turned on (see page 35).

2. Use a strong password that is different to any other passwords you use. If you can't remember it, write it down in code and store it somewhere safe in your home. (See page 76 for more on passwords).

3. If you use your smartphone to access your online bank account, be sure to have a PIN or password set up to lock your mobile phone, so that it's not possible for anyone to use your phone without that PIN/password.

4. Avoid doing online banking on free WiFi services or on a public computer (see page 40).

5. Check your statement regularly and notify your bank straight away if you notice anything strange.

6. Enter the address of your bank's website in your browser (or go to the page via your internet favourites or a search engine). Never click on a link to the website in an email, as this could be a fraudulent site, set up to steal people's details. Your bank will never send you an email asking you to confirm your log-in details.

My bank called and asked for my security details. Is this okay?

Never, ever give out your password or PIN via email or an unsolicited phone call – nobody from your bank will ever ask you for your entire password or PIN. If you're unsure as to whether it's really your bank calling, hang up and ring them back on an advertised number. Either use a different phone to call the bank, or call someone else first to check that the line has indeed been disconnected. Why? Because sometimes a scammer may stay on the phone line and use a recording of a dialling tone to make you think the call has been disconnected. Then, when you think that you are dialling the bank, you are actually still connected to the scammer.

How would I know I'm on a fraudulent site and not the real banking website?

It's rare that this would happen, but it's important to know how to avoid it. As well as checking for the locked padlock/solid key symbol and the https in the web address, which indicate a secure website, be on the lookout for suspicious pop-up windows, and pay attention to the processes for logging in, making payments and so on – are they different from what you usually do? If so, ring your bank – don't log on as normal.

What if I think my details have been compromised or stolen?

Online banks are subject to legal regulations, so you have legal protection if something does go wrong. Always contact your bank straight away if you think you are a victim of fraud – a delay may count against you.

MAKING PAYMENTS

How can I pay for things online, without making a bank transfer?

There are several ways. When you shop online, you will be asked at checkout stage how you would like to pay. Usually you can pay by debit or credit card by entering your details. There is also often the option to pay by PayPal (see page 256). If you're using an online auction site (such as eBay) or a classified ads site, you may also be given the option to complete the transaction offline, by sending a cheque, doing a bank transfer or paying cash on delivery. The most secure method is to pay by PayPal or credit card, so the transaction is tracked.

Is it safe to enter my card details online when paying for things?

So long as you take the right precautions. Think about whether it's a reputable website – do you know the company behind it? Do your friends use it? Is it recommended online by other sites that you use? Next, check that the website is secure by looking for the padlock symbol and https in the address bar. If the website is secure, then it's okay to enter your details. However, avoid making payments, even on a secure site, if you are out and about and using a public WiFi network, to minimise the chance that anyone might 'eavesdrop' on your payment. Pay for things over a secure WiFi connection, such as your home broadband.

Bear in mind that you should never be asked to enter your bank card's PIN when paying online. If ever you are asked for your PIN, do not enter it – and be suspicious of the website. You will almost certainly be asked for the three- or four-digit security number on the back of your credit card, however, and it is fine to type this in.

The shopping website is asking me to create an account before I pay for things – should I do so?

Yes, this can help to ensure that your details are kept safe, because it means you'll need to create a password in order to log in to the site. The site will ask for your name and address, and these will be stored for when you visit the site again. You can usually choose whether to store your card details for next time. You can often pay without entering your card details at all if the site gives you the option to pay by PayPal.

What is PayPal?

PayPal is an intermediary that securely stores your bank and/or credit card details and allows you to pay for things online without those details being revealed to the seller. PayPal is available on many shopping websites as well as private auction sites such as eBay. Not only is it a very secure way to pay (your bank/card details are not revealed to the seller), it's also very quick. And, with PayPal Buyer Protection, you have rights as a buyer to return the item if it's faulty or not as described, and get your money back.

How do I pay through PayPal?

You'll need a PayPal account first, so visit the website to sign up. PayPal puts in place many security measures, so signing up can be lengthy, but it's worth it for the time saved while shopping online, and for the extra security. At the checkout on any shopping site, look for the option to pay by PayPal and select this. Then you just need your PayPal username and password in order for payment to proceed. You can store different methods of payment within your PayPal account (bank account, debit card, credit card) and at the PayPal checkout you get to select your preferred payment option.

Does it cost anything to use PayPal?

It's completely free if you're a buyer. PayPal makes its money by charging a fee to sellers that use the service to receive payments.

What if a seller won't accept PayPal or card payments, and wants to complete the transaction offline?

This situation is usually encountered when using an auction site or classified ads site. It's not necessarily suspicious: the seller could well be genuine – perhaps a private person who does not have the facility to accept credit cards, or else a commercial seller who would rather not pay PayPal fees. In such situations, it is best to arrange to inspect the item before handing over money. Generally, you may prefer to use Paypal whenever the option is there.

Is it safe to buy something from another country?

Yes, so long as the website is reputable it's perfectly secure to make purchases from other countries. Use the same caution that you would with websites from your own country – check it's a secure website, that it has an established reputation and so on. The one thing to remember is that you may not be covered by consumer protection laws that exist in your country. If there is any possibility that you might want to return the item (which could be costly in itself), check the website's own policy on returns, and find out what consumer laws exist in the country you're purchasing from. If in doubt, purchase expensive items on your credit card – most credit card companies refund your money in the case of fraud that is not your fault.

Know your scams

In the online world, as in the 'real' world, there are criminals who will try to con people out of money. But most scams are variations on a few well-worn themes. So long as you know about them, and how to avoid them, you'll be able to bank and shop online safely. The basic law of avoiding scams is this: if it seems too good to be true, that's probably because it's not true.

The phishing scam

The scammers steal your personal details by tricking you into entering sensitive information via an email link. The email could look convincingly like a message from your bank or from another official website. It might say that you need to verify your details or your account will be closed. It might even say you've won the lottery. No reputable company will ever email and ask you to click a link then enter your login details, so never, ever do this. You'll find the website is fake and designed to steal your details. If in doubt, check by ringing the real company on an advertised number.

The money transfer scam

This is when you wire money (via various companies) to a scammer. Wiring money is the same as giving someone cash: you can't get the money back, and it's difficult to trace the recipient. For these reasons, don't ever wire money to someone you do not know. Fraudulent requests might come from an online love interest, someone advertising holiday homes, or even someone claiming to be a friend or relative in trouble. Or someone might ask you to deposit a cheque for them, and then wire them the cost of the cheque. But the cheque is fake, and by the time it bounces, your money is long gone.

The fake cheque scam

You sell something online and the buyer offers to pay by cheque, then sends a cheque for more than the agreed amount and asks you to wire back the difference. The cheque is fake, but as cheques take time to clear, you transfer the change to the buyer before the cheque bounces, at which point you're left out of pocket on two counts (you lose your item and the money you transferred).

The 419 scam

The term '419' refers to the section of the Nigerian criminal code dealing with fraud. But though this trick has long been associated with Nigeria, many of the scammers trying it these days are based in the USA or Europe. The scammer emails and asks you to help facilitate the expatriation of a large sum of unclaimed money in exchange for a percentage cut. Often the request comes with an outlandish tale of how the money came to be available (the very implausibility of the story is part of the scam: it serves to weed out all but the most gullible). The email looks official and the scammer often pretends to be a government employee. You'll be asked to wire a deposit – a much smaller sum than your proposed cut – which will be used to smooth out some last-minute hitch. Once you pay, the scammers take the money and you will never hear from them again.

The credit offer scam

You receive an email or see an advertisement online that says you've been approved for credit. On application, you're asked to pay a fee. You pay the fee – and that's the end of the matter. There is no loan, and no approval. Never pay upfront for the promise of credit.

How do I give to a charity online?

The internet has made it easy to donate to charities. You can go to the website of your favourite charity, where there is sure to be a facility for you to make an online payment – look for a button or menu page that says **Donate**. Another popular way to give to charity is through third-party sites such as GiveNow.com.au. This site makes it easy for people to donate money, skills, time or other resources and services to thousands of registered charities. It can help you find out about a range of different charities across many different fields, and doesn't take any commission.

Are there other ways to give to good causes online?

There are microfinance websites where you can pledge money. One such website is kiva.org, where you loan an amount as small as $25 to help someone anywhere in the world set up a business. This money is made available to people with no access to capital otherwise and you'll get updates on what is happening with your money and the progress made. Kiva takes no fee and is a non-profit organisation. There are other sites, such as kickstarter.com, where you can pledge money for creative projects in need of funds. Kickstarter takes a small fee from each successful project.

BUYING AND SELLING

What can I buy on the web?

Almost anything from valuable diamond jewellery to food or toys. It's just a matter of searching for what you want, either via a search engine or within a reputable shopping website.

Let's start with books. Where's a good place to get those?

As with any item, there are countless resources available online. Most bookstores have an online presence – so you can shop with a company you know and trust. There are also online-only stores, including Amazon. You can buy new books from these sites, and often second-hand ones too.

How do I use an online book store?

It's easy. You can search for the title (or the author or keywords) within the website and you'll be given a list of options, including new and second-hand books. Then:

- Click on the book you want, and you'll see more information about it and may be able to inspect some pages.

- Before you decide to buy, check the cost of postage – sometimes new books come with free postage, so a cheap second-hand book may actually end up costing more once postage is added.

- If you want to buy it, click on **Add to bag** or **Add to basket**, and it will be saved (you can delete it at any point if you change your mind).

- You can add other books or items and then click on the bag or basket icon (often in the top right-hand corner) when you are ready to pay.

- You will need to create an account with a secure password and contact email at this point, or log into an existing account.

- Follow the instructions for paying, and enter in your payment details. Confirm your purchase and you'll be sent an email with your order number (this usually comes through within a few minutes).

Do other websites work in this way?

Yes, they do. You log on, search for what you want (or browse the site's suggestions), and add items to a shopping basket or similar before you pay. Some sites – notably Amazon – have diversified, so you won't just find books but many other items as well: music, DVDs, toys, games, homeware, foodstuffs, tools and instruments, and much more. Some are sold by the company direct, others are sold by third parties. But you order, pay and return items in the same way and through the same website.

How can I compare the prices of items I might want to buy online?

Your best starting point is a search engine. Type in the item you want to buy, and perhaps add the word 'buy' to your search. The search results will then bring up various online shops so you can investigate the price and delivery options they offer. Many shops also have online stores and you may see these coming up in the results.

Most search engines, such as Google, have a dedicated Shopping search facility, so use this to target your search specifically towards online stores. Enter your keywords and search in the usual way, then click on the Shopping link below the search bar. Say you are searching for bicycle accessories. If you search in the usual way, the results will include the Wikipedia page on bicycle accessories and any current news stories. Once you click on **Shopping**, you will primarily see bicycle products that are for sale in your country. The price and stockist (or stockists) are listed underneath each product. Click on the product image to bring up more details of the stockists.

That's brilliant. So I can find the cheapest option pretty much instantly?

You can. But be aware that not all stores are listed on the shopping search, so it's worth doing a general web search first to get a feel for what is available. And, of course, you should only go with the cheapest option if the seller is reputable and you have taken any delivery charges into account. You could also try using a price-comparison website, which compares the prices of goods from various online sources.

What's a price-comparison website?

It's a website where you can compare goods from different shopping outlets. They don't sell the goods themselves, but gather together prices from other websites and provide links so that you can click through to the one you want. Enter 'price comparison website' into a search engine to find these. They are useful for information, but be aware that they don't include every seller and some require retailers to pay to be listed, which narrows the field further.

What about more unusual items – can I get gift ideas online?

Whether you want to adopt a meerkat for someone or buy personalised cufflinks, you'll find all sorts of gifts online. If you're stuck for ideas then browsing online stores is a good way to start, as they generally organise their gifts into categories, such as male, female, children, couples and different age groups. There are also dedicated gift sites that sell anything from gift experiences (a day out paragliding or a spa weekend, for example) to small, novelty presents and personalised gifts.

Where do I go for handmade gifts?

Many small sellers have individual websites, but if you just want to look for unique gifts then a couple of good sites are Etsy, ArtFire and Madeit. Here you can buy (and sell) anything handmade, arts, crafts and vintage items, including wedding invitations, jewellery, knitted clothes, ceramics and craft supplies. They are interesting sites to browse and if you're a person who makes things, then your creativity could make you money (see page 269 for more about selling goods).

If you're a person who makes things, then your creativity could make you some money.

Problem with an item purchased online?

Consumer laws vary from country to country, but if you buy something from an online store in Australia, you generally have the same consumer rights as if you had bought it from a shop (unless you purchased something from a private seller). If an item is faulty, you are entitled a replacement, refund, repair or other type of 'remedy', depending on the problem (unless you were alerted to the problem before you purchased it, as in the case of a 'second'). You should not have to pay the postage on a faulty product. The method for returning items varies from seller to seller so check the website where you bought it for details. If the online store is a retailer with a shop-front, you can usually return the item to a shop rather than by post. A store doesn't have to allow you to return an item simply because you changed your mind about it. However, some stores have their own in-store policy to offer a refund, exchange or credit note for such purchases.

What about my weekly grocery shop? Can I do that on the net?

It's easy to do that online, too. Most major supermarkets offer a delivery service, so if you're unable to get to the store or would rather shop from home, you can browse the website – which is usually organised into lists that match the aisles you find in an actual supermarket – on your computer and have everything delivered to your door. You get to avoid the queues at checkout, there are no fuel costs or carrying heavy bags if you have no car, and no travelling time, just a delivery fee. Many supermarkets have introductory offers with discounts or free delivery for new customers.

Does it take a long time to do a supermarket shop online?

It takes a while the first time. But most sites offer you the chance to create a 'favourites' list (or create one based on your previous shops). This saves you time if you tend to buy the same items on a regular basis, because you don't have to search for them again. And it is simple to search online for particular items – certainly quicker than hunting up and down the aisles. There are usually pictures of the items, so you can be sure that the item you are buying is the exact thing you want.

What if the shop runs out of the things I have ordered?

Some supermarkets substitute something similar if the exact item is not available. It can be tiresome to find you have been given green capsicums when you specifically wanted red ones – but you can usually choose to have nothing if the precise thing you wanted is out of stock. Any substitutions should be listed separately on the delivery sheet, so you can take a quick look and return anything you don't want to the courier.

Of course, another disadvantage of online supermarket shopping is that you cannot select the exact piece of fruit or vegetable that you get. If you are the kind of person who likes to pick up three pineapples and choose between them, or if you always take your parsley from the back of the rack to get the one with the later sell-by date, then you might prefer to limit your online shop to heavy items, pantry items and non-perishables: washing powder, cans of dog food, canned food and breakfast cereals, for example.

How do I book a supermarket delivery – do I have to wait in all day?

No. The delivery times are usually split into slots of about two hours, and at the checkout you choose your desired delivery slot, which can be during the day or even late into the evening. Less popular slots and those a few days away are often cheaper than the next-day delivery slots, so if you can plan ahead you can save money.

AUCTION SITES

What is eBay?

It's an online auction site, where anyone – individuals or small businesses – can sell new and used items. It makes its money by taking a small fee from sellers. Buyers can use it for free to find whatever they want, from pottery to clothing. Goods on eBay can be cheaper than in online stores. And it's a good place to source rare items that are no longer in production. If you have unused items lying around at home you could make a little extra cash by selling them on eBay, and as a buyer you can sometimes grab a bargain if no one bids against you.

How do I buy something on eBay?

You can use the search box on the site to find something specific, or you can browse the site by selecting categories and looking through items. There are two types of sale on eBay: auction items that you bid on and aren't guaranteed to win unless you're the highest bidder, and 'buy it now' items with a fixed price, which you can buy instantly. Once you have a set of search results, you can choose to view both types of sale or just one by clicking on **All listings**, **Auction** or **Buy it now** at the top of the results list.

In order to buy (or sell) something, you need to sign up to the site and create a login and password. Then, for 'buy it now' items, you just select the item you want, click **Buy it now**, and follow the instructions for payment.

How do I bid on an eBay auction?

At the top of the item's page, you'll see a box that you can type text into and underneath that box is text that tells you the minimum amount you can bid, for example, 'Enter 0.01 or more'. If someone has already bid on the item, then you'll be asked to enter more than the previous bid. In the box, enter the maximum amount you are willing to pay for the item. The price will not increase to this amount unless others have also submitted bids up to that amount.

The way it works is that the bid amount increases incrementally up to the ceiling price that you and others have bid. So if the current leading bidder's highest bid is lower than your highest bid, the price will increase by an increment above the leading bidder's maximum, but not right up to your maximum. This system is quite helpful as it means that you don't need to be online as the auction progresses – eBay will bid on the item for you each time someone else submits a bid. You will receive an email from eBay to tell you if you are outbid by someone, so you can go online and increase your maximum if you want.

Are there any good strategies for winning an item?

One useful tip is to log on at the very last minute, just before the auction ends, and submit a bid that's higher than the last price – the other bidders may not then have time to increase their own offer. Another way to win items is to look for those that others haven't found, such as items where the title contains a common misspelling. There are websites that generate common eBay misspellings – fatfingers.com is one such – so you can enter the search term (e.g. 'gardening gloves') and it'll give you possible misspellings ('garening gloves') to bring up items that most people won't find, and where the auction is consequently unlikely to reach a high price.

How do I know whether an item is new or used?

Items for sale on eBay can be new or second-hand. The item listing will tell you this, so be sure to read the details. In fact, always read the details of any listing carefully, as this is your only recourse should something not be as described and you need to send it back. If you neglect to read the details and find out the roll of wallpaper you ordered is actually for a doll's house, you've got no right to return it and get your money back unless the item description wasn't clear about this.

So I can return an item and get my money back if it's not what I wanted?

Not quite. If the item is not as described, or it is faulty and this wasn't made clear on the item description, then yes, you can return it and get your money back – this is easier if you have paid via PayPal (see page 256). But if you receive the item and decide you don't like it, you have no right to return it. However, items have different return terms and conditions, depending on the seller. Some sellers will accept a return if you change your mind, though most individual sellers won't.

Is it best to pay by PayPal, then?

Yes. While you could send a cheque or pay by bank transfer, PayPal is recommended because you have more rights as a buyer in the event that something goes wrong with the sale. If you want to be a seller, it's good practice to accept PayPal as a payment option – because it's naturally very popular with buyers.

I have some things I'd like to sell on eBay. How do I start?

The site can be a great way to make some extra money. But do check that the item is worth selling. It takes time to set up an auction listing and photograph the item, so there's no point wasting your time over something that won't make you much profit or is unlikely to sell at all.

Set up your own online store

If you want to sell goods online, you don't have to go to the bother of setting up your own website; there are many sites that will act as an intermediary for you. They range from huge companies such as Amazon to specialist sites such as Etsy for handmade items. You usually register with the site as a buyer, and then follow a link to become a seller. You will need to come up with a memorable name for your store (make it easy to spell, so that customers can find you) and to upload digital images of your items, which you list on the site with the price and shipping costs. The site will email you when you have an order, and you then pack and post the item while the site handles the payment. You may have to pay a small fee to list each item for sale or the site will take a percentage of each sale you make. You can usually promote your goods on the site for an additional fee, and it is a good idea to publicise them on social networks such as Facebook, Twitter and the like. You'll have to declare any income you make to your country's tax authorities, of course, so do keep a record of any costs as well as the money you make.

How do I check my item's worth selling?

First, search for similar items on the site to see if they have sold. Click **Advanced** next to the **Search** button to bring up the advanced search page. On this page, enter your search term (item title) and then scroll down to where it says **Search including** and tick the box that says **Sold listings**. The search results will now bring up only items where the sale has ended (whether the item sold or not). All successful sale prices are listed in green, and unsuccessful sales (no buyer) are in red. This gives you a good idea of whether or not an item is popular and will sell, and at what price. It will also help you decide under which category of goods you should list it.

I have done the checks. What next?

You need to set up an item listing. If there's a similar item in the results of your research, click on it: under the image of the item you'll see the words **Sell it yourself**. Click on this, and you'll get straight to an online form to begin listing your item for sale. Some of the form will already be filled in with the details of the similar item, which saves you time.

To sell a completely new item, unlike any other available on eBay, click on the **Sell** menu at the top of the page, then **Sell an item** and the online form will load. Follow the instructions on screen. You will need to register with the site and create a seller account, supplying your contact details and the types of payment you will accept before you can list an item.

I'm not sure how to describe my item.

The title is how people will find your item when they search and the first information they will get about your item in the search results. So include likely terms to make it easy to find, and as much useful information as possible to encourage them to click on your item. For example, don't just put 'Black dress', but 'Ladies black party/special occasion dress, size small', or any other descriptive terms that a potential customer might type in.

Put as much honest information as possible to describe your item so that the buyer is left with no questions. If there are any defects such as a small stain on a pair of curtains, or a book with a well-used spine, list them here and explain that they are shown in the photos. The online form will ask if you want to upload a photo (or photos) of your item.

Do I need to bother with the photo?

You have little chance of selling it if you don't. Buyers always want to see what they are being offered – particularly when buying second-hand items. It's a good idea to upload a couple of images, to show the item from different angles. And if your item has any damage you should include more than one photo, the second photo showing a close-up of the imperfections.

Do I have to pay to sell an item?

You do, and you have to pay whether the item sells or not. But if it doesn't sell first time then you can relist the item again for free, and you can adjust the starting price or any other aspect of the listing at any time to encourage a sale. The listing price varies according to the starting price you set (the lower the price, the lower the fee), the category it is listed in and any optional extras you choose when you fill in the online selling form. If your item sells, you'll also be charged a final-value fee, a small percentage of the final price. In addition to this, if you accept PayPal as a form of payment, you'll be charged another small percentage by PayPal. All these need to be taken into account when deciding your starting price.

I don't want to pay. Are there any sites that sell second-hand items for free?

There are several. One is eBid, which charges no fees to list items and gains revenue mainly from advertising. There are also sites that work like the classified ads you find in newspapers. Craigslist is one such site, where you can find and advertise goods, services and even your home.

I can sell my home online?

Absolutely! It's not easy to do on your own, but it's worth investigating and if you can pull it off it will save you a lot of money on real estate agency fees. Craigslist is a free way to put your house on the market privately – but you may not reach many potential buyers that way. You might want to use an online estate agent. You get fewer services than with a face-to-face service, and will have to host the viewings of your home yourself, of course. But if all you want is a virtual shop window in which to display your house, then they're a good option.

What about my car?

If you want to sell your car, consider listing it on a car-sales website and you'll get a wide audience of potential buyers. There's nothing stopping you from listing your car on a general auction site, of course, though there's a risk that you won't get the price you are hoping for.

SAVE AND EARN ON THE WEB

Can I use the web to save money?

Definitely! It's always worth using the web to track down news of sales as well as to find discount codes and promotional vouchers. You can save money on many things you buy – including fuel, haircare, groceries and restaurants. And it is so easy that many people now do it as a matter of course before they buy.

What's the best way to find vouchers?

There are two ways. The first is to sign up to a dedicated voucher website, such as Vouchercloud or Groupon. These sites gather together deals from many vendors. You'll find lists of vouchers and deals, plus discount codes that you can enter at the checkout to save money on certain websites. Some vouchers listed are for online or offline use, so you can print them out and save money in the store. Second, if you know you want to buy something at a specific online shop, it's worth checking whether or not a discount code or voucher is available before you complete your purchase. On a search engine, perform a search with the name of the shop and the keywords 'discount voucher', and you may well find a money-off or other voucher (such as one for free postage) in the search results.

Groupon seems to have deals as well as vouchers. How do these work?

Groupon offers deals every day by email – significantly discounted items and services available to buy for a limited time only. This could be any service or item: a manicure at a local salon, a weekend away, a food processor or sports equipment. Companies use Groupon as a way of advertising their business to Groupon's large mailing list. The deals are dependent on a set number of people signing up and if the number isn't met then the deal doesn't go ahead. To receive deals you'll need to sign up (for free) to Groupon, whereupon you'll receive daily emails advertising the deals. You just might get a shot at a fabulous bargain.

It's worth checking whether or not a discount code or voucher is available before you complete your purchase.

Switch and save

The net makes it easy to compare prices and find the best deals on household bills such as gas, water, electricity and insurance. The key is never to be loyal to a single provider: switch frequently, and do it all online.

Say 'no' to auto-renew

Don't ever let your car, home or other insurance renew automatically when the annual contract is up. Most insurance companies make money by relying on people to take the easy option and accept the renewal quote without question. Usually the renewal price is more expensive than getting a new deal elsewhere, or even with the same company, so shop around every time it comes up. Many insurance companies will give you a quote online when you put in the details of your car. But you can still haggle and play their offers off against each other for the best deal.

Flick the switch

Keep tabs on your energy usage and aim to compare energy suppliers at least once a year. They are all keen to have your business. If you do find a cheaper deal, the energy companies will take care of the switch.

Compare and contrast

Use comparison sites to save time and compare deals all in one place. However, bear in mind that not all providers are available on comparison sites – you may want to supplement your research by making some phone calls to providers or by getting direct quotes from their individual websites.

Get money back

Once you have found the best deal, check cashback websites to see if cashback is available. Compare the cashback price with the best deals to work out the cheapest option.

It's wise to claim your earnings frequently, and as soon as possible, as they aren't officially yours until they're safely in your bank.

It sounds great. Is it really that good?

The main snag is that you can get so keen on the idea of saving money that you sign up to things that you don't really need. Be strict and only sign up if the deal is something that you genuinely want to make use of. If the deal is for a beauty or other personal treatment – massage, teeth whitening and so on – do your own research into the company behind the deal. Sign up only if this is a company you want to do business with.

Any other money-saving ideas?

Yes: use a cashback website every time you make an online purchase. You'll need to create a free account with a cashback site first (if a site asks you to pay to sign up, avoid it). You can earn back significant amounts when buying things such as home insurance, and small amounts on everyday purchases such as clothing, DVDs, stationery, photographs and so on. The cashback will build up if you use the site regularly. Some sites even have a downloadable app that tracks your movements and pays you a small fee just for walking through the door of a shop on the cashback list.

How can I build up cashback?

To make a cashback site pay, you have to get into the habit of checking every time you want to purchase something. Do this by searching the cashback website for the retailer you wish to buy from. If cashback is available, click through to the retailer's website from the cashback site. This click-through is logged, and once your purchase has been made your cashback begins to be processed. It can take a while for cashback to come through, and you'll need to accumulate a minimum amount before you can claim it. You can usually choose to receive it by bank transfer, or there might be an option to take it in the form of shopping vouchers that are worth more than your actual earnings. It's wise to claim your earnings frequently, and as soon as possible, as they aren't officially yours until they're safely in your bank.

I have loyalty cards for quite a few different stores. Can I get something similar online?

If you have a smartphone, you can get rid of many of your loyalty cards and download an app instead – many stores now offer these. You just open the app when you're at the store's checkout, and a barcode scanner will scan your phone when you pay for the item. Similarly, some coffee-shop chains have a downloadable app that you can top up with money and use to pay for your morning latte. Each coffee you buy earns you points, and eventually a free drink.

I don't want my phone cluttered up with too many apps, though.

The good news is that there are also apps that display different loyalty cards in one app, so you don't have to download each one onto your phone separately. Search the app store on your phone to find these – there are plenty of free ones.

Save with QR codes

Have you spotted anything that looks like a square barcode on the window of a shop, back of a book or on an advertising poster, and wondered what it is? It is a QR code – QR is short for Quick Response – and many shops and companies are using them as a way of offering discounts and bonuses. To read these codes, you need a smartphone, and you need to download an app called a QR reader (there are lots of free apps that do this). Then, when you come across a QR code, you simply open the app and hold your smartphone in front of the code to scan it, as if you were taking a photograph. Your phone will then give you the option of loading a website that might contain a discount, a money-off coupon, a loyalty bonus or some other kind of promotion (they can be used as 'proof' that you have visited a particular store, for instance, which may help you earn points). There are many other uses for QR codes. You may see them in magazines or at tourist attractions, for example: scan the code, and you are taken to a site that gives you additional information about the article or the attraction.

Earning extra cash

I've heard I can earn money by doing online surveys. Is that so?

Internet surveys can be an easy way of making some extra cash – just by sitting at your computer. Research companies need people to do their surveys – and they are willing to pay you a fee (albeit a very small one) simply for telling them what you think. All you have to do is sign up and complete the surveys to accrue points; these build up into cash rewards or vouchers that you can spend at specific stores. Doing surveys is never going to make you a fortune, but if you enjoy doing them then the little bit of cash that they make you is a welcome bonus.

How can I maximise my return?

For a start, never pay to do an online survey. If you are being asked for money, then it is never going to be worth your while. Sign up for a few sites – Swagbucks, Rewarding Ways, Ipoll, Ipsos and Global Test Market, for example – many surveys require people to be specific ages, so this will help you access a reasonable number of surveys that you're eligible for. Do spend a bit of time creating your profile as this can influence the surveys that you are asked to do. And be sure to check your email account regularly – surveys are usually operational for a fixed period, and you don't want to miss the deadline.

It's also worth claiming your money as soon as you can – don't leave it in the account. And if you earn vouchers rather than cash, make sure that you use them quickly – many have expiry dates and may become worthless if you hang onto them for too long.

Doing surveys is never going to make you a fortune, but if you enjoy doing them then the little bit of cash that they make you is a welcome bonus.

If you go several months without completing a survey, you could find the emails tail off.

Are there ways of getting extra points?

If you have friends who are likely to be interested in doing surveys too, you can usually get rewards for referring them. There will be a **Refer a friend** or similar link somewhere on the site if this is the case. But check your friend is happy for you to do this and has a dedicated email address – joining these companies can put you in the firing line for spam.

Do I have to do every survey I am eligible for?

No, it is entirely up to you how many surveys you do, and when you do them. You can do lots one month, and nothing the following month. But obviously, the more you do, the more points/rewards you build up. And if you go several months without completing a survey, you could find the emails tail off.

Do I need to declare the money I make?

Money made from surveys is classed as earnings, so you will need to keep a record of how much you make, in case you need to declare it for tax purposes. If you fill out a tax return, you will have to include it; if not, ring your tax office for advice.

Protect against spam

It is a good idea to set up an email account specifically for your survey 'business' – this will stop your usual account from being flooded with survey requests and any associated emails. Always check the privacy policy of any survey website before you sign up. And whenever you do register for a new site, look for the option that asks if you want to have your details shared with other companies – sometimes you have to tick the box if you are happy to have your details shared and sometimes you have to tick if you don't want this – make sure you make the right choice.

A friend does 'mystery shopping'. Is this worth doing to earn money?

It can be, if you have time and are interested in helping shops monitor and improve their customer service. If so, this can be a fun way for you to make a little extra cash and get bonuses such as a complimentary drink or meal. There are lots of mystery shopping websites online, and again you shouldn't sign up unless it's free. As with survey sites, give as much information as possible when you sign up, as some assignments are available only to people of a particular age and so on.

How does it work exactly?

Once you have signed up, you'll start to receive emails telling you of available assignments in your area. Assignments can be popular so you'll need to be quick to respond if you do want to do one. You'll be given instructions about what to do and will have to report back following the task by rating different aspects of the shopping experience. Your expenses will usually be paid, plus you'll earn cash or vouchers for each assignment.

How else can I make money online?

Try entering online contests to win prizes. Many companies offer very good prizes, such as holidays or tablet computers, because it's a great way to publicise themselves (and cheaper than making an ad). This isn't a guaranteed way to make money or win prizes, of course, but if you enjoy 'comping' and have time to enter many competitions then you're very likely to win something at some point.

- You usually enter by filling in an online form, and this costs nothing except time.
- Don't enter competitions that cost money, as there are plenty of free ones out there.
- Make sure you keep track of the competitions you have entered so as not to go in for the same one more than once (for which you might be disqualified). Some contests allow only one application per household.
- It is wise to set up a separate email address for comping, as you'll be flooded with confirmation emails otherwise. It's fine to use the same one as for your surveys (see page 277).
- Don't forget to check and clear out the clutter from your email account, though – you might miss the email telling you you've won!

Index

u

v

w

y

Instant Internet Answers

Writers Zoë Wildsmith, Kim Davies, Charlotte Raveney, Jonathan Bastable
Editor Kim Davies
Art editor Ginny Zeal
Designers Alys Martin, Kylie Mulquin
Consultants Daren Payne, Bill Dawes
Proofreader Ali Moore
Senior production controller Martin Milat

READER'S DIGEST GENERAL BOOKS

Editorial Director Lynn Lewis
Managing Editor Rosemary McDonald
Design Manager Donna Heldon

PICTURE CREDITS

Fotalia: 13, 23, 28, 33, 35, 39, 50–1, 54, 78, 79, 124, 129, 131, 133, 145, 146

Shutterstock: cover, 1, 2, 3, 8, 24, 42, 66, 75, 81, 84, 94, 101 (right), 105, 117, 118, 126, 127, 132, 136, 144, 154, 161, 162, 166, 182, 184, 186–7, 188, 192, 193, 196, 200, 202, 211, 216, 226, 248, 254, 275, globe (end papers and throughout)

Thinkstock: 14, 18–9, 20, 27, 31, 34, 37, 40, 45, 48, 49, 50, 58, 61, 63, 68–9, 72, 76, 77, 82, 89, 90, 91, 96, 98, 101 (top, left), 102, 108, 110, 113, 114, 130, 135, 138, 140–1, 147, 148, 150, 153, 159, 165, 171, 173, 174–5, 177, 179, 187, 201, 204, 205, 206, 207, 209, 214, 220, 223, 229, 231, 234, 235, 236, 237, 238–9, 241, 244, 247, 255, 256, 259, 260, 263, 265, 266, 268, 271, 273, 276, 278, 279

Instant Internet Answers is published by
Reader's Digest (Australia) Pty Limited
80 Bay Street, Ultimo, NSW, 2007
www.readersdigest.com.au
www.readersdigest.co.nz
www.rdasia.com

First published in 2013 in the United Kingdom by Therefore Publishing Limited for The Reader's Digest Association Inc., under the supervision of Pegasus Regional Limited. *Instant Internet Answers* is owned and under licence from The Reader's Digest Association, Inc.

This edition first published 2014

National Library of Australia Cataloguing-in-Publication entry
Title: Instant Internet answers.
ISBN: 978-1-922085-62-7 (hardback)
Subjects: Internet.
Dewey Number: 004.678

Prepress by Colourpedia, Sydney
Printed and bound by Leo Paper Products, China

We are interested in receiving your comments on the content of this book. Write to: The Editor, General Books Editorial, Reader's Digest (Australia) Pty Limited, GPO Box 4353, Sydney, NSW 2001, or email us at: bookeditors.au@readersdigest.com

To order additional copies of *Instant Internet Answers*, please contact us at:
www.readersdigest.com.au
or phone 1300 300 030 (Australia);
www.readersdigest.co.nz
or phone 0800 400 060 (New Zealand);
or email us at customerservice@readersdigest.com.au

Book code: IE 0288/IC
Product code: 041-5387